**Why Am I Afraid to Divorce?**

To be read with care!

Not a book written from a Christian viewpoint but does have some practical suggestions.

**Books in the same series**
Series Editor: Phillip Hodson

**Why Am I afraid to Be Assertive?**
    by Patricia Mansfield

**Why Am I Afraid to Enjoy Sex?**
    by Paul Brown and Chris Kell

**Why Am I Afraid to Grieve?**
by Ann Carpenter and Geoffrey Johnson

# Why Am I Afraid to Divorce?

by Jane Butterworth

Series Editor
**Phillip Hodson**

Fount
*An Imprint of* HarperCollins*Publishers*

Fount Paperbacks is an Imprint of
HarperCollins*Religious*
Part of HarperCollins*Publishers*
77–85 Fulham Palace Road, London W6 8JB

First published in Great Britain
in 1994 by Fount Paperbacks

1 3 5 7 9 10 8 6 4 2

Text copyright © 1994 Jane Butterworth
Preface copyright © 1994 Phillip Hodson

Jane Butterworth asserts the moral right to be
identified as the author of this work

A catalogue record for this book is
available from the British Library

ISBN 0 00 627672-5

Printed and bound in Great Britain by
HarperCollinsManufacturing Glasgow

CONDITIONS OF SALE

This book is sold subject to the condition that it
shall not, by way of trade or otherwise, be lent, re-sold,
hired out or otherwise circulated without the publisher's
prior consent in any form of binding or cover other
than that in which it is published and without a
similar condition including this condition being
imposed on the subsequent purchaser.

All rights reserved. No part of this publication may be
reproduced, stored in a retrieval system, or transmitted,
in any form or by any means, electronic, mechanical,
photocopying, recording or otherwise, without the prior
permission of the publishers.

# Contents

| | |
|---|---|
| PREFACE | vii |
| INTRODUCTION | 1 |
| 1. For Better, For Worse | 3 |
| 2. Can It Be Saved? | 19 |
| 3. Your Partner | 29 |
| 4. Breaking the News | 41 |
| 5. You're Not Divorcing Your Children | 55 |
| 6. Money | 69 |
| 7. Why Am I Afraid to be Single? | 79 |
| 8. Afterwards | 95 |
| USEFUL ADDRESSSES | 115 |
| FURTHER READING | 119 |

# Preface

Whatever the moral crusaders may say, no one enters into divorce lightly. There isn't an epidemic of bored husbands and wives who decide one weekend to divorce because there's nothing to watch on television. On the contrary, everyone loses something in a divorce, especially the children.

On the other hand, there is a clear NEED for divorce and healthier divorcing practices in any modern country. Some relationships are doomed to disaster from the outset, for predictable reasons, and the participants need to find the means to go their separate ways.

It was always so. Three hundred and fifty years ago, life expectancy at birth was thirty-two years – death in effect did a lot of the divorcing that today we expect the law to undertake. Then in the early nineteenth century, as soon as public health measures were introduced and people began to live longer, the clamour for divorce reform began.

The 'natural' tide of divorce can be gauged from what happens when the law does get liberalized – the rate has risen by 500 per cent in the UK since 1960; the rate has risen similarly in Italy since this freedom was introduced, and the same is predicted to happen in Ireland when they finally remove their outmoded legal ban.

# WHY AM I AFRAID TO DIVORCE?

In 1993, life expectancy in the West is practically eighty years for both sexes, and it's possible for a marriage to last more than half a century. For some, that is just too long.

But divorce still carries a mixture of stigma and sense of failure, it threatens people with loss of home and identity, and can set up a chain reaction of grief and depression. It's these difficulties that Jane Butterworth's admirable book aims to address. She deals with divorce and all that surrounds it in a straightforward manner, saying the things most people who find themselves in this situation are too afraid to think about. It is non-patronizing but it is also not a textbook. Overall the author deals with the couples and surrounding adults rather than the more common focus which is on children (though Chapter Three does cover the main childcare issues). Children are the prime victims in a divorce but that doesn't mean the adults are having a wonderful time.

What I especially like about Jane's book is the mix of real-life examples coupled with her own experience of men and partnerships. We see why people get married, and early on she supplies a test list to show if YOUR relationship is in trouble and what you can do about it. The nitty gritty question is faced – the whole of Chapter Two helps you to decide whether a poor relationship can in fact be saved. So please try to read as far as page 35 at least. Equally important, Jane explores the 'wrong' reasons for couples to stay together.

Once you have decided to divorce, how should you tell other people? The author suggests sensible ways you can communicate your intentions to partners, family and friends. Breaking bad news successfully is an art not easily mastered even by doctors and nurses – so Jane's words here are especially valuable. With a look at the important subject of domestic violence, the divisive issue of money and a consideration of the spiritual and religious impact of divorce, Jane concludes by suggesting that divorce always causes grief – and requires a natural period of mourning. With this guide, however, the fears involved can be faced and survived by those who have to make the journey – currently 160,000 couples in Britain every year.

Phillip Hodson

# Introduction

Most couples wed with the expectation that their marriage will last for the rest of their lives, but the sad reality is that over a third of all marriages will end in divorce.

Divorce is almost always a tragedy for everyone involved but particularly for the children, whose needs are often overlooked during this unhappy time. On a practical level, divorce can mean a drop in income and reduced living standards for one or both partners, homelessness, and debt. On an emotional level, it can mean grief, pain, anger, bitterness, sadness and confusion. The decision to separate is not usually a mutual decision which has the agreement of both partners, and accepting that a marriage is finally over can be hard.

If your marriage is dead there is little point in ruining your lives by staying together, as no amount of work will revive a dead marriage. A divorce can be traumatic and painful, but it can also be positive. It marks the beginning of a new phase in your life, and you can emerge from it stronger than you were before.

Deciding to end your marriage is one of the most important decisions you'll ever make, and it's a decision you must be absolutely sure about. Of course you're afraid. If you make the wrong decision it could affect the rest of your life. This book will help you face those fears. It is not a book which encourages you to divorce. It's a book which gives you information, and the confidence to be able to make the decision that is right for you.

*It's a book which should give you hope for the future.*

CHAPTER 1

# For Better, For Worse...

> What is it men in women do require?
> The lineaments of Gratified Desire.
> What is it women do in men require?
> The lineaments of Gratified Desire.
>
> WILLIAM BLAKE

Marriage is one of the most important steps a couple can take. It's a public declaration of mutual commitment and the final step in a courtship, and to underline its importance most of us mark our wedding day with a joyful celebration. It also continues to be an immensely popular institution, despite the rise in cohabitation: if current trends continue, 79 per cent of men and 83 per cent of women will have married by the age of fifty.

## WHY DO WE MARRY?

The romantics among us believe we marry because we fall hopelessly in love, but the reality is a little different. We marry for a variety of reasons. Security. Companionship. Because there's a baby on the way. To get away from home. To spite our parents. Because someone thought enough of us to want us to marry them. Because we mistook sexual desire for love. Because we don't want to be left on the shelf. Because we believe ourselves to be head-over-heels in love with someone. Or perhaps because we really are head-over-heels in love with someone.

There are dozens of reasons why people marry, and sometimes love doesn't enter into it. This is not a bad thing as long as both partners are clear about why they're marrying, and each can fulfil a mutual need. An attractive and charming woman might marry a wealthy man she doesn't love for the security of his money. The wealthy man might marry the attractive and charming woman because he's proud to be seen with such a personable companion. Providing they both carry on wanting each other to fulfil those roles and providing they both carry on fulfilling them, they can be perfectly happy living together without love.

Whatever the reason, few people get married thinking anything other than their marriage will last for ever. Marriage is assumed to be a commitment for life, whether it is solemnized by the church or legalized by the state. Of course there are those who have doubts on their wedding day. Some may even realize they're making a mistake and call the whole thing off, but making that sort of last-minute decision takes a lot of courage. Most people go through with the ceremony even though they may be riddled with uncertainty, because of pressure from their parents or because they don't want to let their partners down.

There are also couples who are coerced by parents into marrying against their will, usually because a baby is on the way. Unhappily, these marriages are most at risk, particularly if the couple are in their teens, and most have little chance of lasting. What marriage cannot do is make a bad relationship good. Marriage brings an emotional pressure that can strain a relationship that isn't absolutely secure to breaking point, and the couple who marry after cohabiting claiming their relationship will remain unchanged are deluding themselves.

Even those who marry reluctantly often convince themselves that all will be well once they're married because somehow things will change. The notion that it could all end in the divorce court is the very last thing on our minds when we dress up in our finery and head for the church or register office. Jim had grave misgivings about his forthcoming wedding, but because he was unworldly and immature he put it down to nerves. It didn't occur to him he might be making a mistake:

> I was a naive and inexperienced boy who'd spent most of my life studying. Barbara was my first girlfriend. We didn't go to bed because I believed then that sex should only be within the context of a marriage. So when she suggested we get married, it seemed the logical step. My mother encouraged it because Barbara came from a local wealthy family and she saw our marriage as a chance for me to climb the social ladder. I was uneasy, even on the morning of the wedding, but I didn't know why. My father was dead so there was no one to talk to about it and I couldn't bring myself to raise the subject with my friends. I thought it was pre-wedding nerves and things would work themselves out, but on our honeymoon I realized the whole thing was a disaster. We had nothing in common, sexually, emotionally or intellectually, and not long afterwards I realized that things weren't going to get better and what the heck was I going to do about it. At the time, I was the vicar of a small country parish so divorce was unthinkable.

Marriage is often seen as a panacea for all that is wrong with a relationship. Some couples believe all their problems will disappear as soon as the marriage vows are made. The truth is that if something's a problem before you marry it will be an even bigger problem after. Minor irritations you can cope with as a single couple can become major difficulties following the first heady flush of the honeymoon has worn off and you have to contend with day-to-day living.

## WHAT CAN GO WRONG?

If you are reading this book the chances are you're not happy with your marriage and you're probably wondering what has gone wrong. Just as there are many reasons to marry, many things can cause a marriage to founder. The commonest cause given for the breakdown of a marriage is unreasonable behaviour, which usually means incompatibility. If a couple marry young, while they are still in the process of development and discovery, they can sometimes develop in different directions when they mature and eventually grow so far apart they find it impossible to live together. Some were incompatible right from the start and should never have married, but they became so swept up with excitement, romance and sexual desire, they either ignored the warning signs or mistakenly believed that love can overcome incompatibility.

It can be easy to mistake sexual desire for love, particularly if you're young. Sexual desire can be so strong it can fool two people who have nothing other than that in common into thinking it's all that's important in a relationship. Maybe they realize they haven't a lot in common, but they believe they can change each other when they're married and that all their problems will be miraculously resolved. Too late, they often realize the gap between them is so wide it can't be bridged, as Janet discovered:

> I met and married Rob in the space of three months and I think I knew at the time it was a daft thing to do. He was an actor and I felt so attracted to him it was almost like an addiction, and all I wanted was more, more, more! We're both very volatile people and I knew from the start we had fundamentally different views, but I didn't think it mattered, I thought it just meant we'd never have a dull relationship. The first big argument was about whether or not we should marry in church. I've always thought of myself as a Christian and marrying in church was important to me. Rob was an atheist and he flatly refused. He said he'd feel a hypocrite if he married in church. In the end I gave in to him, and justified it to myself by thinking well, it's us who're important, not where we marry. I was sure I could make him more tolerant in the future, because he was tremendously intolerant of anyone else's viewpoint. But I couldn't, and that difference between us proved to be the first of many. Our relationship stopped being stimula-

ting and started to become scratchy and ill-tempered, and I started to long for a dull relationship, if dull meant not arguing. It took me some time to realize we actually had nothing in common, nothing at all, and the beginning of the end was when the sexual attraction between us waned because then there was nothing to hold us together at all.

Teenage marriages, particularly if the wife was pregnant when they married, are at particular risk: a bride who marries in her teens is twice as likely to become divorced than a bride who marries in her mid-twenties. Inexperience, immaturity, isolation, low income and accommodation problems are all recurrent features in the breakup of teenage marriages. Teenagers often marry with unrealistic expectations of marriage, and when the fairy-tail romance they were expecting doesn't materialize, the reality comes as such a shock the couple simply can't cope with it.

An affair, even if it was only a one-night stand, is for many couples the biggest crisis that can happen in a marriage. It can break up even a relatively strong marriage, although in many cases infidelity is a symptom that all is not well with a relationship rather than the cause of the problems. Infidelity can cause powerful feelings of rejection and jealousy in insecure people. All they can think of is their partner's affair and try as they may, they simply can't come to terms with it. It preys on their mind so much they are unable to close the chapter and move on, and the only way out of their torment is to finish the marriage.

Jealousy can have an equally destructive effect. Sometimes one partner's self-dislike and lack of self-esteem is such they find it impossible to believe their partner can be faithful to them, and they become obsessionally suspicious and possessive. They cause a scene if their partner so much as speaks to a member of the opposite sex. They check up on them, listen in to their phone calls, go through their pockets looking for evidence of real or imagined affairs. Eventually they succeed in driving their partner away, or they break up the marriage themselves rather than live with the constant mental torment.

A marriage can be destroyed by sexual problems, when the partners are sexually incompatible, or when desire for each other has evaporated or was never really there. Or when the relationship is one-sided, with one person always giving and the other taking, although this doesn't necessarily lead to a marriage breakdown: many couples can live quite happily in this way unless the giver realizes one day how little he or she is receiving from the relationship.

A marriage can be destroyed by one partner's abusive behaviour, and marriages such as these often last far beyond the call of duty. Sometimes fear prevents a woman from leaving a violent husband, but more often than not it is apathy. The abuse she has suffered has desensitized her to such an extent she believes such behaviour is normal, and hasn't even noticed her marriage is dead. Some remain in violent relationships for ever, while others only leave the marriage when something happens which jolts them back to reality, such as an affair. With Louise it was glimpsing the future:

> I felt powerless, almost institutionalized when I was married to Vic. I did what he wanted when he wanted it because I knew if I didn't he'd get nasty. So I just switched off and became like a zombie. I think I loved him when we got married but he was different then, still had a nasty temper but he never used to hit me. But then he started drinking and getting these violent rages and I just lived my life trying to keep me and the children out of his way. One day he banged my head against the concrete path over and over again and I can remember our neighbour shouting at him over the wall and all I could think of was why doesn't she mind her own business. Do you know when I finally decided to go? I was waiting for a bus one day and I saw this elderly couple walking down the road hand in hand, obviously in love and happy in each other's company. And I realized that's how marriage should be, not like us. And I knew if I didn't get out I'd never have a chance to experience that sort of tenderness.

Falling in love is a heady, exhilarating experience. We want to constantly touch the other person, our bodies yearn for them, we want to be with them the whole time, we're in an almost constant state of sexual excitement. It's a magical, unreal, unbelievable time ... and of course it doesn't last. We wouldn't be able to stand the pace if it did. Sooner or later it settles down into a more tranquil *being* in love, and that's what some people can't accept. They're hooked on falling in love. They want their relationships to be like that for ever. They can't accept that it just doesn't happen like that and so they give up on the relationship altogether and move on.

## ARE YOU IN LOVE WITH A FANTASY?

When we're teenagers, many of us nurture fantasies of the person we want to marry – fantasies which are fed by television advertisements portraying 'ideal' families and reinforced by reading romantic fiction. Our fantasy lovers are always attractive and usually wealthy, given to making romantic gestures, charming, good-tempered and caring – in short, they're not the slightest bit like real people. Most of us grow up and move on from that but some people don't, and when they meet partners they are unable to see the real person, only the fantasy. Marriage to them is a continuing fairytale romance, and so when they marry they have completely unrealistic expectations.

When reality fails to live up to the fantasy it can be a tremendous shock. When a partner loses a job and there's not enough money at the end of the week to buy food, when a baby comes along and is hungry for attention, when the marital home consists of a high-rise flat in a block whose walls are covered in graffiti, when clothes have to be bought from charity shops, when clubbing is something only your single friends can do, these are all aspects of marriage with which even those with their feet firmly on the ground would find it hard to deal. For those with unreal expectations of marriage it can be devastating, as Natalie discovered:

Why did I marry at the ridiculously young age of 18? Because when I met James I fell for him. Or rather I thought I did. Maybe I was just swept along by the fact that he was attracted to me, and as he was ten years older than me and he had an

XR3I, I was flattered he'd even noticed me. He was also the first person I'd slept with which added another dimension to our relationship. I was the first of my friends to marry, and we had the wedding I'd always dreamed of – a beautiful romantic dress, a huge reception, the works. I lost my job soon after we married but it didn't matter, I was having fun. It was like playing house. His dad gave us the deposit on a house for a wedding present and I used to spend all day in this little terraced house polishing, like a kid in a Wendy house. The novelty began to wear off when we began to have money worries. The car had to be sold, and he started to blame me, said I should have got another job. Things weren't going too well in the business he and his dad ran and we had to cut back, but I hadn't a clue because I'd never had to manage money before. I'd go shopping for food and we'd run out of money in the middle of the week and he'd hit the roof. We never had any money to go out, the house began to look like a tip because I began to hate housework and he never lifted a finger, and we had row after row. The strain became unbearable. I wanted to be out enjoying myself, not stuck at home watching TV every night. The last straw was when I got pregnant and he went mad, said we couldn't afford a baby and I ought to have an abortion. I was horrified – no way would I get rid of it and I think that's what dealt the death blow to our marriage. I looked at him one day and realized I didn't love him, didn't even like him very much. I think you could say I came down to earth with a bump.

Natalie had unreal expectations about marriage, which left her totally unequipped to deal with the problems that arose when money became tight. The shattering of her illusions left her feeling angry, resentful and cheated. Had she been more clear-sighted about what lay ahead she would have been aware of the possible pitfalls, and she might have been able to ride out the storm – but then had she been more realistic she might not have married James in the first place.

## CHANGES

We go through life in a constant process of change and development, depending on our circumstances, character, environment and outside influences. The rate at which people change varies, and a lot depends on their time of life. A woman who is content to stand still during her childbearing years might in middle age suddenly want to forge ahead and develop her potential. A domineering man who married a submissive woman who was content at the outset of the marriage to remain in her husband's shadow may find himself some years later married to an assertive woman who wants to be a success in her own right.

Problems occur in a relationshp if a couple develop in different directions and grow apart from each other, because eventually they can outgrow each other completely. The submissive wife who becomes assertive, for example, may cause her husband to feel undermined. Couples may start off as equals with shared interests, but something happens which causes one partner to change to such an extent they leave the other behind. David gradually realized after nearly twenty years of marriage that he and his wife Jenny no longer had any points of contact:

> When Jenny and I married I was selling cattle feed and she was a secretary in the office. We were happy enough together, and I thought she'd make an ideal wife and mother because she was a very caring person and she liked looking after me. I wasn't particularly ambitious and neither was she, all she wanted was to be a housewife and mum, which was fine as far as I was concerned. She got pregnant right away and we were reasonably happy until I fell out with my boss and lost my job. I was so sick of the way I'd been treated I decided to set up my own business, undercutting my former employers. It was a tremendous success, and grew from strength to strength and I realized I had a talent for making money. Our lives started to change. We bought a new house, and I started to mix with the sort of people who wouldn't have given me the time of day in the past. I joined the golf club, bought ponies for the kids and became friendly with the local hunting

set. I suppose you could say I became a pillar of the local community. But Jenny hated it all. She hated the new executive house on the private estate, she felt uncomfortable with my new friends, she said they made her feel inferior because she wasn't very good at making conversation. Never mind that she had the money to dress in the best clothes, to hire a nanny, to do what she liked. She still had the small-time mentality we both started off with and eventually we grew apart so much we were like two strangers. We parted ostensibly because I was having an affair with someone whom I've since married, but the reality was that the marriage had been over for years before that happened because Jenny wouldn't move on. It was tragic really, and I felt guilt for a long while. But there was nothing I could do about it.

Not all couples grow apart from each other in such an extreme way as David and Jenny. In a happy marriage each partner acknowledges the other as a growing and developing person and they manage to grow and develop alongside each other. Some marriages stand still, with each partner apparently coming to an unspoken agreement not to move on, in case it rocks the boat and threatens their relationship. They're probably not even aware of what's happening, and if they realize their marriage is anything less than wonderful they certainly don't think it's bad.

## RETIREMENT: A DANGER TIME

Retirement can be a time of great fulfilment to some couples, but for others the changes it brings to their way of life can cause a lot of problems. If a wife has never worked she might find her husband's constant presence an invasion of her territory. A man's status is determined by his job, and when he retires he may feel he's lacking a role in life. Perhaps, too, the marriage has had problems which have not been addressed. When one or both partners were working it didn't seem to matter so much because work provided both of them with an escape route, but when they find themselves at home all day with a partner from whom they may have grown apart, it can be difficult to adjust. It's a time when many couples are forced to examine their marriages, and discover them wanting. When Joan's husband Malcolm took early retirement she had no alternative but to acknowledge the truth about her marriage:

> If I'm being honest I've been dissatisfied with my marriage for years. I know why – it's because my husband Malcolm isn't the man I wanted him to be and I suppose he never has been. It takes time to realize truths like that, or perhaps I've managed to avoid facing up to it before because I didn't see much of him. His job meant that he had to work very long hours and he used to get home very late at night, and I wanted the sort of husband who'd be company, someone I could do things with. He wasn't like that. He was made redundant when he was fifty-three, and he eventually took a part-time job which meant he was around every afternoon. This would have been fine if we could have developed interests together but we've no interests in common and if he's not playing snooker he's lying around the house getting in my way. His early retirement has aggravated all the problems between us which have niggled away at me throughout the years and they are slowly coming to a head. But what's the answer? The idea of separating and creating a new life for myself at my time of life is unthinkable.

It's human nature to take the easy option, and if the thought that our marriage is less than happy or that our partner is a different person to the one we married ever crosses our minds we tend to ignore it, make excuses for our situation or rationalize it, unless something forces us to take notice. We tell ourselves that we can't hope to be blissfully happy the whole time and that all marriages go through bad patches, which is true enough – but in a good relationship we can hope to be blissfully happy *some* of the time, and you should be able to remember when your marriage *wasn't* going through a bad patch. But you can only put off facing facts for so long: the nagging feeling of discontent, if not attended to, will grow louder and more persisent over the years until you reach a point when you just cannot ignore it any longer.

Look at the marriage of Tasha and Jake. Tasha, on the face of it, seems to have everything: a husband who buys her expensive presents. Two loving and beautiful children. A comfortable home. A good circle of friends. A secure job, even if it's not very exciting. But she's bored and feels neglected. The years go by and she tries to ignore the nagging insistent voice inside her telling her she's unhappy, but eventually the voice becomes so loud she sits down and asks herself why she's not happy. She starts to think. She remembers all the times her husband has undermined her and the various times he's been unfaithful over the years. She'd like to become a mature student and do a teaching course but when she tentatively mentioned it to him he laughed at her. She starts to feel angry and resentful. The more she thinks about her marriage the more she realizes she's discontented, unhappy and no longer loves her husband. But having faced up to it she's afraid - afraid that the problems attached to ending her marriage - moving out, finding somewhere to live, living in reduced circumstances, being alone, emotional pain for herself and the children - would outweigh the benefits of being able to do as she wants. So she tries to ignore for as long as she can the insistent little voice which has now started to tell her she ought to end her marriage, until the time comes when she has to face up to the problem.

## FACING UP TO THE PROBLEM

Fear frequently keeps men and women in a marriage they both know can never work, despite attempts to save it. Admitting your marriage is over is hard. The repercussions are painful. Living an empty but comfortable existence very often seems preferable to rocking the emotional boat, which is why so many people keep the lid on their discontent and refuse to face up to the truth.

There is a certain appeal in not asking for trouble. Most of us shy away from the prospect of emotional pain and turmoil, so if your marriage isn't happy you don't want to delve too deeply in case you open a Pandora's box from which all the evils of your relationship will fly out. Our natural reaction is to ignore something as catastrophic as that until something happens which forces us to acknowledge it.

Most of the divorced people I spoke to told me they could remember quite clearly the first time they thought about divorcing their partner, and all of them dismissed the idea as being too shocking to contemplate. They eventually took the decision to divorce only after many months or even years of deliberation. Divorce is certainly not a step anybody undertakes lightly. It's a long-drawn-out process which can be emotionally hurtful, financially devastating, and can have serious long-term consequences for any children involved.

Being forced to acknowledge there's a problem is a lot harder than if you'd faced up to it voluntarily, as Len discovered:

Things had been bad between us, we seemed to spend most of our time screaming at each other and I'd had a couple of relationships on the side. I was in the army and I was away a lot and one day I came home unexpectedly and there she was in bed with another chap. I'd often wondered what people do in those sort of situations, but all I did was wait downstairs until he'd got dressed and scuttled off. Then the row began, and all these things which had been unspoken for so long, all the pent-up anger and emotion, came tumbling out in a poisonous stream. I think what really shattered me, really convinced me that the marriage was finished, was that she was having her period at the time, so they obviously had a really intimate relationship. Thinking about it now I can see that we'd both ignored the fact that our relationship was crumbling away and if things hadn't been brought to a head in the way they were, maybe we'd still be together, which is a terrible thought.

Acknowledging our marriage isn't working is hard enough for most of us but for those whose religion plays an important part in their lives and believe that marriage is for life, it is almost intolerable. Jim, the clergyman mentioned earlier, had to face the fact that his ten-year marriage to his wife Barbara was on the rocks five years ago.

> I was very unhappy, but I just couldn't countenance the fact that we might split because I couldn't face the thought of not living with the children. I'd always been close to them and absolutely adored them. Divorce was unthinkable, something that wasn't an option. I had never envisaged my marriage wouldn't be for life. I had taken it for granted that it would, no matter what happened, but when things got so bad that we came to a mutual decision to part I had no difficulties. I suppose pragmatically because I could see no point in a relationship with no love which seemed to be very destructive for everybody concerned, including the children. Reconciling it with my religion wasn't a real difficulty. Far more difficult than sinfulness and going against God were the feelings of failure. The Church authorities seemed embarrassed when my marriage broke up, and I did get pretty angry that nobody from the Church offered any sort of support or encouragement or even broached the subject. There was just one vicar, a friend of mine, who I talked to because I thought I should resign; it seemed hypocritical to remain as a priest. He was very encouraging and said don't do anything hasty. Just because you're divorced, maybe you can be of help to others who are in the same position, or divorced people who are finding it difficult to stay in harmony with their faith. I've always had a strong sense of love of God and think that this was a saving grace, because if I had been more orientated as many people are to a God of justice I might have felt differently.

We are only human. We make mistakes and sometimes we fail. It doesn't mean we are bad. Acknowledging the mistake often causes less hurt and damage than ignoring it, and hoping things will sort themselves out. When a marriage is completely dead – that is, when a couple feel absolutely nothing for each other, no hate, no affection, just complete indifference because any feelings they had for each other disappeared years before and they are staying together only because they are too apathetic to finish the relationship – nothing will revive it, and the longer the couple stay together the more soul-destroying it will be.

## ASK YOURSELF:

- Has marriage been a disappointment, different to what you expected?
- Do you stay with your partner only because of the children?
- Do you feel trapped by your marriage?
- Do you hate your partner?
- Do you feel indifferent to your partner?
- Do you feel a gap has widened between you since you first married?
- Is your partner violent?
- Do you feel you've got nothing in common any more?
- Do you distrust your partner?
- Does your partner resent it when you have any sort of success?
- Are you bored by your partner's company?
- Is your partner obsessively jealous?
- Do you feel that you do all the giving and your partner does the taking?
- Do you feel undermined by your partner?
- Would you have married someone else if you could have your time again?
- Do you feel sexually indifferent towards your partner?
- Do you and your partner ever talk about your relationship?
- Is your partner the same person you married?
- Do you constantly feel attracted to other people?
- Would you be relieved if your partner walked out tomorrow?

If you've answered yes to more than a couple of questions, your marriage is in trouble. If you've answered yes to more than half a dozen your marriage is on the skids. And it's time for some very deep thinking.

CHAPTER 2

# Can It Be Saved?

Marry, and with luck it may go well
But when a marriage fails, then those who marry
   live at home in hell.

EURIPIDES

Having faced up to the fact that your marriage is in trouble, the next step is to see if it can be saved. That means having difficult and uncomfortable conversations with your partner. It may mean seeking help. It could mean agonizing choices have to be made.

It's right to be afraid of divorce. Divorce is not something we should rush into as a spur-of-the-moment emotional response to a problem. It *hurts*. It's emotionally painful and can have far-reaching consequences for your children. It usually leaves people – especially women – a great deal poorer. Feelings of hurt pride, failure and disappointment are common.

Of course not everyone responds to a divorce in a negative way. For some it can be a relief, a positive step forward. It depends on whether you are the instigator of the divorce, whether you have actively chosen that path. For although when a couple marry both of them are involved in planning the wedding, when a couple divorce it's usually a decision taken by one partner against the other's wishes. The exception is the handful of cases when both partners acknowledge the relationship is over and realize that the only sensible option is to part.

It goes without saying that the partner who doesn't want the divorce will suffer the most, especially if the news is completely unexpected, as it was to Sally:

> We'd had our problems, sure – I was pretty sure he'd had an affair a couple of years before but it seemed to be over and things were a lot better. With hindsight I can see a number of things pointed to it but I'd ignored them. Our youngest daughter Suki had been born with a heart condition and she had to have endless operations, and I was too busy worrying about her to think about what was wrong with us. I knew things with Patrick weren't so good but I thought it was the strain of Suki being in and out of hospital. One day I was sitting at home sewing and I thought he was reading the paper when all of a sudden he put down the paper and said, 'That's it, I want to leave, our marriage is a sham, for years there's been nothing there, I don't love you and I want to leave because I'm in love with someone else'. To say I was stunned is an understatement. I actually didn't believe what I was hearing. I thought he was joking. I had absolutely no idea he felt like this. And when it sunk in that it wasn't a joke the shock was almost like a physical injury, as though he'd stuck a knife into my heart.

If you ignore the warning signs that your marriage is in trouble, when you are forced to face up to the problem it's often too late for the marriage to be saved. Sally had no idea Patrick was so unhappy because he'd bottled up his feelings and refused to talk about his discontent, until a new relationship forced him to speak out. It's arguable that Patrick and Sally's marriage could have been saved if he'd voiced his problems earlier, if she hadn't ignored the warning signs, and if they'd sought some sort of help.

Relate, the former Marriage Guidance Council, see 50,000 individuals or couples each year whose marriages are in trouble. After counselling, around half of those couples stay together and their marriages are saved. It could be argued that the fact that they sought counselling in the first place suggested they were keen to save their marriages, but this is not always so: some couples go to Relate wanting confirmation that their marriage is beyond salvage.

Women usually make the first approach, probably because women have always been encouraged to talk about their innermost feelings and so they seem to find it easier to talk about emotional issues. Men are more likely to think they should be able to solve the problem themselves, and some may be afraid to talk about their feelings or find it very uncomfortable if they're encouraged to do so, because they've been conditioned into believing it is somehow unmanly.

How helpful is marriage guidance counselling? Most people who are experiencing relationship difficulties are unhappy and confused, and talking to a sympathetic, experienced professional who won't take sides often enables you to see things more clearly. Counselling can help a couple discover ways in which their relationship can be improved but it cannot always save a marriage - indeed, some couples in the process of counselling realize their marriage cannot be saved. It cannot work miracles, although some couples seek it expecting that it can. Some people go for counselling hoping for 'permission' to part, or one partner goes hoping that counselling will enable the other partner to see the marriage is over. In a number of cases people go for counselling hoping the marriage can be healed and restored, but gradually come to see that it's not only not possible but that divorce is almost certainly their best option.

## WHAT CAN YOU EXPECT?

Counsellors will be supportive, but give little direct advice. Their aim is to help couples work out their own solutions to deal with the problems that have arisen, to take their own decisions, and to look at how they relate to each other and the problems this is causing in their marriage. A counsellor cannot change reality or make choices for you, but what they can often do is shed some light on to a confusing and often distressing situation and help you to be realistic about the choices you have. If you do end up having to separate they can help you do so with less bitterness. Relationship counsellors certainly don't try and force you to stay together – only you can make that decision.

'You're trying to save a relationship which is important to you, your partner, grandparents, parents, children, and parents-in-law. You're not just talking about your own emotions but a whole interconnecting network, and the idea that this is worth looking after and doing the best you can for is a very positive one, very sensible and adult,' says Renate Olins, director of London Marriage Guidance.

'48 per cent of the couples we counsel are unmarried, but have been living together for some time. Some of our most useful work lies in enabling people to see more clearly that they cannot go forward in that relationship, that they don't want to marry each other – or certainly one of them doesn't.

'Living together just isn't the same. If it was, people wouldn't get themselves all convoluted trying to organize themselves with contracts and arrangements and shared mortgages, where with one stroke of the pen they could be married and have a conventional contract. Most are either in a state of transition into marriage or in a state of transition into splitting up – there are very few people who don't end up getting married, who go on living together for the rest of their lives.'

Some couples have unrealistic expectations about marriage guidance counselling. Natalie made an appointment with Relate in a last-ditch attempt to save her marriage:

I persuaded James to come with me because things had got so bad between us we were barely speaking. He was very half-hearted about it. I can realize now, although I didn't then, that our marriage was totally dead. We'd left any attempt at patching things up far too late. There just wasn't anything left, but neither of us could admit it. It was a last-ditch attempt to see if a third party could help, but to be honest I don't think either of us wanted to save our marriage. We just thought we ought to try because I was pregnant. Heaven knows, I didn't want the baby to start off life in a one-parent family. Also I thought that maybe seeing a counsellor would help push us one way or the other, which in fact it did. We saw this very pleasant woman who was very fair. She intervened and asked each of us to comment on what the other had said, and although James thought she was taking sides because she said she could see my point of view, she wasn't. It was hopeless, though. She told us if we were annoyed about something to try and speak about it to each other, but it was too late. I couldn't speak to him and he couldn't speak to me. The gap had grown so wide that we were like two strangers living together, resenting each other, wanting each other out of the way. We didn't go back again, but it made me realize that all hope was lost and that I had to face up to the fact that we would part.

Relationship counselling usually serves some purpose, even if it's only to make you think through the consequences of a divorce. If you are in a position to do so, you should always think about what you will lose by being divorced and what you hope to gain, what there is in the marriage that's still important enough to you to be worth hanging on to, and whether there is any hope of change to make it possible. Says Renate Olins, 'For divorce to bring with it the benefits one hopes for I think it has to be thought through and digested and planned with at least as much care as you would plan a wedding. Particularly when there are children.'

If people divorce because of a particular problem but don't do anything about that problem, the problem is still going to be there after the divorce. If, for example, you want a divorce because you can't cope with the responsibilities of marriage, you're going to experience similar problems with other relationships. This is where divorce counselling can be helpful: 'If you don't understand enough about why you're divorcing, how can you learn very much from it?' asks Renate Olins. 'Most people who get divorced in their thirties will have other relationships, and if you can learn from it you can feel you've done the best you can and maybe do better next time around.

'Why am I afraid to divorce? is something we'd test out in counselling, to find out whether or not it is a fear of the unknown or something more. They may have genuine misgivings about divorce and all that it brings with it, including very importantly the issue of children and access and visiting if the marriage does break up. A lot of practical arrangements have to be made. Counselling is about exploring the emotional hinterland that is making it difficult to make those arrangements. If you have reached a point of adequate communication then you'll be able to make the arrangements. But what often gets in the way are feelings of bitterness, resentment and betrayal. Counselling can defuse those emotions by gaining a better understanding of where they come from.'

Divorce is never as neat and tidy as some people believe, or would like it to be. If a couple have terrible difficulty living together they're likely to have equally huge problems in parting: 'Whatever drew you together was something very significant and it doesn't go away and actually never goes away,' explained Renate Olins. 'It may become outweighed by other things – you may be drawn to a man by, for example, his optimism and energy but you become disillusioned with him because of his unreliability and infidelity, and so the scales tilt but the optimism and energy will remain. You may meet someone else who is reliable and faithful and less exuberantly optimistic and energetic, but he really looks after you and loves you, and on balance that's what you need. You say, I can't cope with that man, the hurt and suffering that relationship causes me is too much – the point being that you don't go from black to white, you go on being drawn to similar aspects in people. It's like buying clothes, you always look for clothes in the same colours and so it is with people.'

For a marriage to be saved there has to be something there to save, even if it's only the tiniest flicker which can be breathed back into life. Perhaps the partners are compatible, but are not getting on for various reasons. There has to be some degree of mutual affection, respect, trust and friendship. Sometimes the gap between the partners is so wide nothing can bring them together, and that's not always obvious without counselling. Furthermore, both partners must not only want that marriage to be saved but be prepared to work at it, to tackle their problems head on.

## RECONCILIATIONS

Reconciliations can and do succeed, and they often seem to work better if a period of time has elapsed before the couple get back together again. But – to repeat – they need to be worked on. It's hopeless moving back after a couple of months because you don't fancy life on your own, or because you're fed up with sleeping on other people's sofas; pointless hoping for a return to what you had before things started going wrong, if all you do is move back home and expect all your problems to have vanished. The problems which caused the split in the first place must be addressed, or the reconciliation will be very short-lived. If the reconciliation is to succeed you must redefine your relationship positively – your previous relationship is dead and this must be a new relationship. Don't forget, too, that you'll probably have to rebuild your social life as well, as friends and family will have taken sides one way or the other after you separated.

Some families cannot accept a reconciliation, especially when relations between parents-in-law and sons- or daughters-in-law were none too cordial to start with. A friend of mine divorced her husband, to the delight of his mother, who'd always disliked her. They eventually got back together again, but her mother-in-law refused to have anything to do with her, even after she went on to have three children with him. They have been happily remarried for fifteen years, and she still refuses to speak to her.

## MAKING THE DECISION AND TAKING ACTION

According to research, 73 per cent of marriage breakups are initiated by women, that is, they're the ones that do the leaving. It seems that women are not only less likely than men to stay in a dead marriage but they can cope more easily with a divorce. One reason could be that they are, in general, not afraid of talking about their feelings and acknowledging their emotions, whereas many men have been so conditioned into believing that emotions are something only women have they often stay in a relationship they know to be unhappy because they are unable to talk about their problems, and don't know what to do to put things right.

Lack of confidence is one reason why many people are afraid to take action. They don't think they can survive alone and prefer instead to sidestep the problem by resorting to temporary solutions. Some couples have a baby, in the hope it'll draw them together, or perhaps one of them has an affair. Tactics like these are in fact more likely to put the final nail into the coffin of the relationship rather than to spice it up. It's not the things you do that you end up regretting, it's the things you *don't* do. If you stick around in a dead marriage because you're too frightened or lacking in confidence to make the break, the odds are you'll reach a point in your life when you'll regret it – and by then it may well be too late.

I'm sure you can think of opportunities that have presented themselves at various times during your life of which you failed to take advantage, and now you regret not doing so. Perhaps it was a job you turned down because it meant moving away from your family. Or marrying someone your parents didn't like. Or having an affair when the opportunity arose. Or going on to further education. Or buying a particular house. Or starting up your own business. All of us must be able to think of at least one occasion when we wish we could rewrite history.

Whatever it was, the chances are you didn't do it because it involved taking a risk. There was a chance you could have lost money, a job, or the friendship of your parents, and you weren't prepared to take that risk. People who never take risks rarely lose, but neither do they know the exhilaration of winning when a risky manoeuvre comes off. They spend their lives thinking, 'If only I'd done things differently, I wonder what would have happened?' But they'll never know because they never tried.

Ending a marriage usually involves taking a risk. You might find you've made the wrong decision, and once started, divorce proceedings can be hard to stop. But it also might be the most positive thing you've ever done in your life. Thinking about ending your marriage is frightening – a lot more frightening than *actually* ending it. The unknown always is. No wonder most people teeter on the brink of taking the decision for a long time, terrified of taking the plunge until there's no alternative.

There is usually a breaking-point or even a series of events which leads up to a breaking-point when something snaps, and one or the other partner realizes that the marriage is over. It might be something dramatic, like discovering your partner has been having an affair. It might be something as trivial as finally realizing your partner bores you to death when he greets you with the same ritual he's performed for the last twenty-five years. The breaking point in my first marriage came when I came back from a weekend away to discover my former husband had had a party in my absence, and the guests – half of whom he didn't know – had spray-painted the loo, stolen money and broken an ornament I held dear. Don't ask me why these events finally enabled me to see the writing on the wall – writing I'd steadfastly ignored for ages. All I know is that from that moment, ending the marriage was the only option as far as I was concerned.

Below are some common fears about why people can't bring themselves to end their marriages. See how many apply to you.

- I can't afford the maintenance.
- I can't afford to live on maintenance.
- I don't want to move out of my nice comfortable home.
- The children will suffer.
- I don't want to hurt my partner.
- I'm afraid of my partner.
- My parents will go mad.
- I'll never meet anybody else.

- Society doesn't want to know a single parent.
- Better the devil you know.

In the next few chapters we'll be looking at how to cope with these very justifiable fears.

CHAPTER 3

# Your Partner

It is not the lie that passeth through the mind, but the lie that sinketh in and settleth in it, that doth the hurt

FRANCIS BACON

If you've shared your life with someone for any length of time, the chances are you won't want to hurt them any more than you have to – after all, there was once a time when you loved and cared for this person more than anyone else in the world. But things have changed. Maybe they've changed so much you've decided you don't want to share your life with them any longer, but because you once had strong feelings for them you are reluctant to take action you know is going to cause pain. Few of us are cruel enough to enjoy hurting those we care about, but by trying to protect your partner in this way you may miss opportunities to save the relationship.

If you keep your feelings to yourself for fear of hurting your partner, the problems will mount up. Eventually they'll become insurmountable, and when that happens you'll be forced to speak out. By then it will be too late to mend the marriage and you will have hurt your partner far more than if you'd been honest.

As we have observed something often sparks off a confrontation, such as the discovery that one partner has been having an affair. Learning that your marriage is in trouble in this way can be devastating if you've had no warning of any problems. Janet realized she'd made a mistake in marrying Rob soon after she married him but couldn't bring herself to talk about her feelings with him for a long while:

> I'd been unhappy for ages and I'm sure Rob wasn't happy either, although when we finally did get round to talking about it he said he hadn't realized the problems were so serious, he thought we quarrelled and argued so much because we had a lively relationship! I even left him once - briefly - but he still thought things were basically okay. That made me realize what different expectations we had about marriage. I still cared for him but I realized more and more I couldn't live with him. Then I met Barry, and I knew almost as soon as I met him he was the one for me but I was frightened to tell Rob. He's always said the one thing he couldn't stand was being deceived and I knew I was deceiving him by having a relationship with Barry, but I put off telling him because I knew how much it would hurt, and I suppose I didn't want him to hate me. I thought he couldn't live without me, either on a practical or emotional level, which was absolutely daft. Then one day he saw me with Barry and he was absoluted gutted. He'd had no idea anything was wrong with our marriage other than the usual ups and downs, as he put it. That was when I regretted not telling him I was unhappy long before things got that bad, as it would have saved him a lot of pain. It might not have saved our marriage - I don't think anything could, as I don't think I should have married him in the first place - but at least he could have grown used to the idea gradually rather than have everything blasted at him in the way it was. It caused a lot of acrimony between us for a long while.

Be honest. If you're not happy with your marriage and the

reason you haven't voiced your discontent is because you don't want to hurt your partner, how much of that concern *is* concern and not guilt? It's easy to pretend to yourself you're acting out of consideration whereas you really feel guilty.

## DESPERATE MEASURES

Your reluctance to tackle the problem head on may be justified. Some people are not above using emotional or actual blackmail in order to hang on to their partner. Common threats are, 'I can't live without you. If you leave me I'll kill myself.' They are so desperate they don't realize that far from reviving a dead relationship, emotional blackmail merely ensures the relationship's final demise.

It's hard to handle threats like that. You can explain that a one-sided relationship is no relationship at all, that it would be demeaning to both of you if you stayed in a relationship through pity, and that their self-respect would be in shreds if you did, but if they're insecure or possessive enough to want to hang on to you at any price they're not going to hear what you're saying.

Most people who threaten suicide only do so to make their partners feel guilty and afraid, but there are those who might be emotionally unbalanced enough to actually carry out their threat. Unless you're absolutely sure, you should take suicide threats or attempts seriously, without giving in to them. They should be taken seriously because sometimes people take what they think is a safe amount of pills to frighten or to spite their partner, or to seek attention. They don't really mean to kill themselves. What they don't realize is even a dozen paracetamol pills can be fatal, and some of them really do end up dead.

This doesn't mean you have to stay with a partner because you're frightened of what he or she will do to themself if you leave, but you should be watchful and act with sensitivity and tact. The crisis time is usually in the few days after you have announced you are leaving, or immediately after you've gone. Be concerned and show your concern – let your partner know that just because the marriage hasn't worked doesn't mean you don't care. If you're worried, persuade your partner to call the Samaritans or make an appointment with a counsellor or doctor. Contact friends and family to ensure your partner isn't alone – those who have sympathetic and supportive people around them don't usually commit suicide.

There is no easy way of telling someone you no longer want to remain married to them. You can't help but inflict pain, and there's no way round it. No matter how tactfully you dress up the words, you are in effect saying you'd rather be on your own or with someone else than with your partner, and that's hard to take. None of us likes rejection, although it may be less wounding if the news comes as no surprise, or if your partner has been thinking along similar lines. If you suddenly announce out of the blue that you want a divorce to a partner who is unaware of any problems, the shock will be incalculable.

It takes courage to tell your partner you want to end your marriage. Some people don't have that courage, and let their partner know in a letter after they've left. Some have good reason to want to avoid a direct confrontation: if a woman is married to a violent man she is likely to provoke a violent physical reaction if she tells him she wants a separation, and her safest recourse is often just to walk out. But it's the emotional reaction that some people can't face, and their guilt and shame can lead them to dodge their responsibilities altogether and quite literally disappear without a word. They leave behind shocked and bewildered partners.

Mary knew things were bad between her and Jon, but whenever she tried to raise the subject he wouldn't talk about it and so she felt at a loss:

He found it hard to talk about his feelings because he was embarrassed. I think he thought it was unmanly. But we muddled along okay and he loved the children so I thought we'd get over the bad patch. Then one day he didn't come home. It was just before Christmas, the presents were all wrapped and stacked in the spare room, and we'd planned to go to my folks on Christmas Day. When he wasn't home by midnight I was demented, I thought he'd had an accident. I called the police and phoned the hospitals – nothing. The next day I reported him missing and eventually they traced him to a house not far away from where we lived. He'd moved in with this woman, he'd been seeing her for about six months and I'd had no idea. I was just shattered – it was Christmas Eve, he'd been involved with planning our Christmas together and yet all the time he'd known he wasn't going to be there. What made it harder to bear was that his mother had known about it all but she hadn't thought to tell me. He told me he couldn't tell me because he hadn't wanted to hurt me. What he really meant was he was too ashamed to face me. I felt like dying of grief. The fact that he was so unfeeling, so cowardly that he couldn't even tell me to my face he wanted to leave was the cruellest blow of all.

## STANDING FIRM

Guilt and a reluctance to inflict pain are not the only reasons why a lot of people dread telling their partners the truth. Sometimes it's because they're afraid they won't be strong enough to withstand the outpouring of emotion the news is likely to provoke, because unless you are very hard-hearted or your partner has treated you cruelly, this can be hard to resist. Don't let yourself be swayed by an emotional reaction. You haven't taken the decision to end your marriage lightly, and if you allow your partner's distress to change your mind you're probably only postponing the inevitable.

Early on in their marriage Janet had realized marrying Rob was a mistake and it became clear to her that whatever happened, their marriage just couldn't work. She decided to leave him, and planned her departure meticulously. She found a flat which she arranged to share with a girlfriend and prepared herself to tell him:

I thought it would come as no surprise to him because we had such a stormy relationship. We'd even talked about divorce in the past, albeit when we were having one of our frequent and highly emotional fights. On the Sunday morning I told him I was going and he promptly burst into floods of tears and begged me to stay, and I very nearly did. He told me we belonged together, we had a special relationship, and I forgot all the fights, the hurt, the sadness. All I can remember is his terrible grief and I walked out of the door with a suitcase and the cat basket and feeling so, so miserable. He was crying, horrible racking sobs, and I could hear them as I walked down the path. I went to stay with my parents until I could move into the flat, and I spent most of the day in tears. I couldn't bear the thought that he was so unhappy because I cared a lot for him, even if I couldn't live with him. So when he appeared on the doorstep a couple of days later at seven o'clock in the morning and dramatically announced that he'd been sitting on the station all night waiting for the first train, that he couldn't live without me and that I just had to go back to him – what could I do? I went. He was an actor, don't forget. No matter that none of our problems had been resolved. No matter that I'd left my friend with the flat in the lurch. I went because I couldn't resist the emotional tug. It was the stupidest move I ever made, because I just let both of us in for another year of misery until I met someone else and fell in love with him, and ended up going for good.

Janet gave in to Rob because he played on her sympathies. She put his feelings above her own and went back because she didn't want to hurt him any more, but all she did was hurt him twice over. Had she not allowed herself to be persuaded back she would have spared both of them a year of emotional turmoil, and spared Rob the humiliation of discovering she was having an affair. They could have both used that year to come to terms with the loss of their marriage. Instead, she prolonged the agony.

## THINKING ABOUT YOURSELF

Realizing that at the end of the day it's YOU who are important is difficult if you've spent a lifetime trying to please others. This particularly applies to women, many of whom have been brought up not to be assertive, and as a result they have never taken responsibility for themselves or their feelings. Some have never recognized they have needs and wants independent of their partners. They spend their married lives being compliant and agreeing to do things they don't really want to do because they don't want to upset their spouses.

Inside, they might be seething with frustration and resentment, but they can't bring themselves to say what they want, or think or feel clearly and unequivocally. This can lead them to stay in a marriage they want to leave, simply because they can't be assertive enough to say so.

Assertiveness means:

- Taking responsibility for yourself.
- Recognizing your own needs.
- Respecting yourself.
- Saying clearly how you feel and think.
- Asking for what you want.
- Expressing your feelings.
- Having the right to be treated with respect.
- Being able to change your mind.
- Having the right not to take responsibility for other people's problems.
- Having the right to make mistakes.

You may argue that all this sounds selfish and uncaring, that it's all about *me* and what *I* want. In fact it's all about choice. You may well want to put the wants and needs of your partner or children first, but it's important to recognize you have a choice. Some women don't have that choice. They take on other people's problems, particularly those of their partners, because they feel they have to, or because they're talked into it, or because they're pressurized and made to feel guilty, not because they choose to. This means they're very often exploited, and they end up doing things they don't want to do and saying yes when they mean no and feeling angry, frustrated and resentful as a result. This can make it hard for them to extricate themselves from relationships.

If you have decided you want to end your marriage, it's important to tell your partner clearly and directly, so there can be no room for misunderstanding. Don't be aggressive or indirect. Stick to what you've said, repeating it if necessary over and over again. Don't feel guilty about saying no if your partner tries to change your mind with emotional blackmail. Janet put aside *her* feelings and wants and needs when Rob asked her to go back to him, and she did what *he* wanted, even though she knew she was making a mistake. Had she been assertive she would have done what she thought was best for her.

## 'HOW CAN HE COPE WITHOUT ME?'

Some women stay in a marriage they long to leave because they think their partners won't be able to cope on their own. They cook, wash and clean for their husbands because they wrongly believe they are incapable of fending for themselves. 'He'd starve if I wasn't there with the supper on the table each night,' they say. 'He'd go to work looking like a tramp if I wasn't there to iron his shirts. He'd live in a pigsty if I wasn't there to clean up after him.' And the fact that so many men walk straight into another live-in relationship after a divorce seems to bear this out.

I had a friend who was doing an Open Univerity course, and she was going to opt out of the essential summer school because she believed her husband and two children couldn't cope for a week without her. Eventually, after a great deal of pressure from tutors and fellow students alike, she agreed to go – but not before stocking the freezer with food for every day she'd be away, and arranging for someone to come in and do the housework.

Women who mother men in this way avoid taking responsibility for their own lives, but believing they are indispensable gives them a feeling of worth and self-esteem. After all, it's the one area of their life for which they are still responsible. The truth is that most men can cope perfectly well on their own if they have to, and you're kidding yourself if you believe differently.

It's not just women who believe their partners won't be able to cope without them. Men who have dominated and overprotected their wives and allowed them no degree of autonomy, may feel, often with some justification, that they would find life difficult on their own. Indeed they do, but inevitably they manage if they have to. Betty had never had to take a decision throughout her married life, so the prospect of life alone was daunting:

> It was me who took the decision to divorce but it was what he wanted. He'd been having a relationship with someone from work for months, and I'd often said to him, why don't you go? He said it was because he couldn't leave me, I'd never be able to cope. I think now that was just an excuse although at the time I believed him. I had a part-time job but I could never live on the money I earned. We had no children and I was forty-three, and I knew I'd have difficulty finding anyone else. He'd always done everything – decided where we wanted to go on holiday, what colour to paint the sitting room, what car to have. I didn't even know where to pay the bills. I'd never made any decisions during our marriage and taking the decision to end it was the hardest thing I'd ever done. When I finally did it I bought a flat with the divorce settlement and what I found most difficult was that suddenly it was all down to me, I was the one who had to make the decisions. I decided what I had for breakfast, or watched on TV, or wore, and it took me a long time to have the confidence to make those decisions.

If you are reluctant to end your marriage because you feel your partner won't be able to manage without you, you are still emotionally dependent on your partner. You can't break away not so much because you're worried about your partner's wellbeing but because you're still relying on him or her for emotional security. Of course some women find it hard to manage money or carry out household repairs, and some men find it hard to cook or do the housework. Of course some people will find it hard at first to manage on their own, but when a couple separates there is usually an army of people ready with support and practical help to both partners, so it shouldn't remain a problem for long.

## THE ABUSIVE PARTNER

Men who batter women generally do so because they suffer from low self-esteem. It makes them feel powerful and counteracts their feelings of worthlessness if they live with someone weaker than themselves, particularly if that someone is afraid of them. Often they hate themselves and so they take out that hatred on those closest to them. They are afraid of giving and receiving love, and see their partners as possessions. They usually guard their possessions jealously, and don't want to lose them.

It's unsurprising, therefore, that some women stay married to violent partners, because they are too terrified to leave. Some have every reason to be terrified. Violent men faced with the prospect of losing their partners don't usually accept the situation meekly, and some have been known to hunt down and murder them. If you live with a violent man and you think your life may be in danger if you tell him you've leaving him, don't do it. Just go, without any warning. It's the one time when disappearing without trace is the most sensible thing to do.

Women in violent marriages are prisoners, and as well as being justifiably afraid of being physically harmed, they are also often afraid of coping alone because years of abuse have taken away any self-confidence they may once have had. Louise was married to a violent man for eleven years and it didn't occur to her for a long while that she needn't put up with this, that she could leave him:

> When it finally occurred to me to leave him I was too frightened to do it right away. He'd put me in hospital three times and I threatened to leave him once after he'd hit me with a baseball bat, and he said if I did he'd kill me. I believed him. So I put up with the beating and the verbal abuse until one night something snapped. I'd already decided to go but it was taking that final step. In the end he made it easy for me one night by banging my head repeatedly against the wall with his hands around my neck because I'd burnt his dinner. He was drunk. He'd already smashed me in the face with his fist and knocked out three teeth and I suddenly thought, why am I

putting up with this? And I remembered the happy couples I'd seen, the wives whose husbands respected them and cared for them, and it was as if I could suddenly see clearly for the first time. I grabbed the kids, who were cowering in a corner, and ran out into the night, no shoes on, mouth bleeding, to my friend's place round the corner. The police arrested him and took him away. They were terrific, they gave me the number of a women's refuge. While I was there I realized the reason I hadn't left years before was because it hadn't occurred to me that I could. Living with him had dulled my feelings and sensitivities that much. I bumped into him a few weeks later and I was terrified what he'd do, but he started to cry and said he was sorry he'd hurt me. That was when I realized I wasn't frightened of him any more and it was a liberating experience.

A woman who stays in a violent relationship also suffers from low self-esteem. Deep down she believes she must deserve such treatment, that it's her fault her partner behaves in this way, and that she's not worthy of being treated with gentleness and respect. Maybe her father abused her mother, and she's grown up thinking this is what marriage is all about. If she's never known any other sort of man, she may fear worse treatment at the hands of another, and even a husband who physically abuses her gives her a degree of emotional security. She probably also hopes that he'll change, which of course he won't. Violent men tend to get worse, not better. If you're in a violent relationship, get out of it. Now.

## THE JEALOUS PARTNER

Jealousy is a common cause of marriage breakups, but it can also keep a couple stuck in a dead marriage. The man or woman whose spouse has been repeatedly unfaithful during the marriage will feel more jealous in the marriage than out of it, because the act of leaving will relieve the jealousy. But for those who've had no cause to be jealous but whose insecurity is such that they suffer from illogical feelings of possessiveness and jealousy, the notion of anyone else having their partner is anathema to them. They might not want him – but they don't want anyone else to have him, either. Part of the reason why Deborah found it so hard to break away from Glyn was because she couldn't bear the thought of him with anyone else:

> I was so insecure during my marriage to Glyn that even after I'd decided, right, this is it, I've got to leave, the one thing I couldn't tolerate when I thought about it was the thought of him making love to someone else. I'd imagine him with all these women and I'd feel physically ill at the thought. I'd even met someone else I was really fond of, and he adored me and the children, and Glyn and I had grown so far apart we used to either ignore or verbally abuse each other. I knew the best thing to do would be to end our marriage because there was nothing there for me, but my gut reaction said no. Eventually I went to see a counsellor and she helped me realize that it was my insecurity which was making me hang on and eventually I was able to break away.

Few people are lucky enough to be able to end their marriages without at least some degree of emotional trauma or conflict, and children caught up in the process of their parents' divorce can suffer a lot of pain and sadness. But the short, sharp pain of a breakup is usually easier to bear than the long-drawn-out agony of a dead marriage – for everyone concerned.

CHAPTER 4

# Breaking the News

Though it be honest, it is never good
To bring bad news

**WILLIAM SHAKESPEARE**

In theory, the only people who need know when a couple decide to separate are the couple concerned, their children, parents and in-laws. In practice, it's not so straightforward. There is a whole army of interested, concerned or just plain nosey people to whom you'll have to account – friends, acquaintances, teachers, even employers. It's particularly important to tell teachers because they can play a major role in helping your children through this difficult time, and will be understanding if your children's behaviour or standard of work suffers as a result.

Breaking the news that your marriage is over can be distressing and uncomfortable for you and the people who care about you, particularly if you feel sad and emotional when you talk about it. Your friends will be concerned. They'll ask questions and make assumptions if they don't get answers, and for that reason it's often better to tell them the full story rather than leaving them to draw their own conclusions. Some will take sides, and if one of you is leaving to live with a new partner you're likely to distance or even alienate yourself from many of your mutual friends.

## GET IN FIRST

The reaction to the news depends on whether you're the initiator of the separation, and whether or not it was unexpected. If relations had been publicly bad between you and your partner, people may well have been expecting it. The people who care about both of you are likely to be shocked, sad, angry and emotional. You'll probably find yourself having to console them when it's you who's in need of comfort and consolation.

A lot of people tell their family and a few key people initially and leave it to them to spread the news. If you do that it's crucial you get in first so it's your side of the story that's doing the rounds, not your spouse's. Their version of events is likely to be somewhat different to yours, particularly if you have instigated the divorce. If you're not on good terms you're likely to be vilified and blamed for all that was wrong with the marriage. Another option is for you to break the news together, but this can only be achieved if you are still on good terms or one of the few couples who decide mutually and amicably that the marriage has run its course and they're better off apart.

Having others spread the news for you has advantages. It saves you from having to tell people who are not important in your social scene but who need to know (mothers doing the school run, for example) but the story will inevitably become distorted in the telling. It's possible, too, that without an opportunity to ask questions people will make their own, often negative, interpretations. By the time the news has done the rounds of your family and friends the story will sound somewhat lurid. If you can tell the tale in an unemotional way without slandering your partner, but making it sound as though you've given it your best shot and tried as hard as you can, you'll have a definite advantage if friends are forced to take sides.

A friend of mine saved himself a lot of emotional turmoil and embarrassment after he and his wife separated by sending out a printed letter baldly stating the facts without any embellishment. This rather clinical approach did at least mean that neither he nor his wife had to go through the often upsetting business of telling people face to face, and that people were given the facts and not rumour. He also managed to deflect much of the concerned outpourings of friends, which, though well-meaning, can be hard to cope with in the immediate aftermath of the separation.

## TELLING THE PARENTS

Breaking the news to your parents is particularly difficult because they are emotionally involved in your marriage, especially if you have children. How they react depends on what your marriage meant to them, but they're likely to view your separation with dismay. They face losses of their own – grandchildren, a son-in-law or daughter-in-law, family holidays and Christmases. They may well have close bonds with your spouse's parents and brothers and sisters. They are likely to put pressure on you to change your mind, and it can be hard to resist unless you are absolutely confident you are doing the right thing.

How you break the news to your parents can make a difference. If you break it gently and ease them through it with the least amount of fuss they'll suffer minimal distress, but, if you're angry and hostile towards your partner and involve your parents in a prolonged and bitter slanging match you'll make it extra hard for them.

However bitter and angry you feel, try not to criticize your partner to your parents. If you've got children it's in their interests that everyone remains on good terms. Be as unemotional as you can, allow them to think calmly and make their own judgements. They'll need your reassurances that you can cope and you're okay. They'll want to know what sort of part they're likely to play in the future lives of their grandchildren.

Most people are sad when they report the breakdown of their marriage, but some are not. It will help if you are serious rather than euphoric, grave rather than tearful, and calm rather than emotional when you tell your parents the news, because they'll feel uneasy if you seem too happy, and distressed if you seem too miserable.

For some parents, the news comes as no surprise. Roger:

> I phoned my mother up and said, 'Guess what?' she said, 'She's left you. I always knew she would. What would you like for supper tonight?' She'd always hated her and when she left as far as my mother was concerned it was as though she'd never existed.

Some parents blame themselves: they'll wonder if it was something they did or said. Should they have been nicer to your partner? Did they set the wrong example because they haven't been that happy? If they'd brought you up differently, would you have been a better husband or wife?

If you've fallen in with your parents' wishes throughout your life and allowed them to dominate you, you probably find it hard to be assertive with them, especially if you are the instigator of the separation. It took Sue a year to find the courage to tell her parents:

> We nearly split up a year before we did. I wanted to after I found Tim'd been carrying on with someone. But I just couldn't face it – my mum and dad thought he was brilliant. I sometimes used to think they loved him more than me, and I thought they'd blame me and make a terrible fuss. So I tried to sweep things under the carpet because I couldn't face the hassle. A year later he upped and went. At first my mum tried to make out it was all my fault and I'd driven him to it, and I got really angry. It was a while before they came round to seeing that he wasn't the blue-eyed boy they'd thought.

If you initiated the separation your parents will probably encourage you to try a reconciliation, unless your partner was violent or abusive. They'll remind you of your responsibilities to your children, they'll point out how badly off you'll be financially, and they'll make you feel guilty by reminding you of all they've done for you. They may threaten all sorts of things in an effort to get you back together again because they're desperate: after all, they have a vested interest in your marriage continuing.

Of course parents are important, but at the end of the day all that really matters is that you do what you think is right. Even if you upset your parents, after the dust has settled they'll probably side firmly with you, regardless of whether or not they see you as the 'villain' of the piece. Some try to remain neutral for the sake of the children but if the separation becomes acrimonious they are liable to become hostile towards their estranged son- or daughter-in-law, and put the blame squarely on their shoulders. After all, blood is thicker than water.

If you're sure you're making the right decision, you should be able to withstand any amount of pressure, even if parents make misguided attempts to patch things up. One of my newly-separated friends returned home to her parents' house where she was staying to find her estranged husband sitting there waiting for her. Her mother had phoned him up and persuaded him her daughter was keen to go back with him, left a key out, and arranged for him to turn up when everyone else was out. Needless to say it was a futile, if well-meaning, exercise.

Here is a checklist of your parents' likely reactions. Have your responses ready.

| REACTION | RESPONSE |
| --- | --- |
| 'What about the children?' | 'The children will be happier away from the bad atmosphere there's been lately.' |
| 'You should never have married him/her. I knew it wouldn't work.' | 'It was my decision. We were happy for a while.' |
| 'What a waste of a life.' | 'On the contrary, I'm on the verge of a new chapter of my life.' |
| 'All those wasted years.' | 'No experience is a bad one if you can learn from it.' |

| | |
|---|---|
| 'What will the neighbours say?' | 'Who cares? It's my life.' |
| 'You needn't think you can come back here.' | 'I don't want to. I need some time alone.' |
| 'You can come back and stay with us.' | 'I don't want to. I need some time alone.' |
| 'How could you do this to us?' | 'It's my life and I'm doing what I think's best.' |
| 'How will you manage?' | 'Well, I hope.' |
| 'Why on earth didn't you do it sooner?' | 'I wanted to be sure.' |
| 'I never liked him/her anyway.' | 'Things were good for a while.' |
| 'How can you do this to him/her?' | 'I'm doing what's best for both of us.' |
| 'He/she can't cope without you.' | 'Then it's about time he/she learnt.' |
| 'Better the devil you know.' | 'No it isn't.' |
| 'What about the children?' | 'In the end they'll be better off.' |
| 'Would you like me to talk to him/her and see what I can do?' | 'No!' |
| 'You're being very selfish.' | 'Selflessness is not always best. Doing what's best for me is important, too.' |

## YOUR IN-LAWS

Few people are lucky enough to keep on good terms with their in-laws. Many in-laws have an uneasy relationship with their son or daughter's spouse, which has its foundations in jealousy or rivalry. Divorce can bring these suppressed feelings to the surface. If you've no children there's no reason why you need have anything to do with your in-laws after you separate, unless you enjoyed a particularly close relationship with them that both of you want to maintain. If you have got children, it pays to remain on reasonably cordial terms with in-laws despite the coolness which is likely to develop between you. Whatever the reasons behind your marriage breakdown, they're likely to blame you. Even if their son or daughter had innumerable affairs, gambled, drank away the family allowance, and physically or mentally abused you, the chances are they'll still think you drove them to it!

But they *are* your children's grandparents and if they've been good for the children, grit your teeth and try and bear any criticism. If you're the custodial parent, they can provide you with a much-needed break in the school holidays by having the children to stay, or by baby-sitting if you want a night out. Most important of all, they can give your children some much needed stability and continuity at a time when their lives have been disrupted and they're likely to feel very insecure.

Reassure them that no matter what has happened between you and their son or daughter, you'd still like to remain friends. Assure them they'll still be your children's grandparents no matter what happens, and they'll be able to carry on seeing them. Say something like, 'I really value our relationship and so do the children. You've been like a mum and dad to me and I'd hate to lose all that. I know that things can't be the same between us but for the sake of the children if nothing else, I'd still like to carry on seeing you and be your friend.'

Some grandparents you're better off without. There are those who try and avenge themselves by using their grandchildren – particularly younger children – as weapons, as Jo discovered:

Geoff and I divorced when Kelly was a year old, and since she was two she's been spending Saturdays with him and his parents. She didn't know him at all before then and although he left us when she was a few weeks old he had the nerve to apply for custody. I think he was put up to it by his mother. He didn't get anywhere and now I think she's trying more subtle and insidious ways of getting Kelly off me. Kelly's started coming back from seeing her saying she doesn't like me, she wants to live with her Nan, and she was frightened of sleeping in our house because of witches. It doesn't take much to work out that she must have got all that from Geoff's mother. I felt so angry and helpless too – how could I stop her? I went to see her and she was hateful, told me that I was an unfit mother and she'd do anything to get Kelly off me. In the end I had to stop her seeing her and told Geoff he could only see Kelly round at my place in future. He's threatening to go to court about it.

Not all grandparents want to keep contact with their grandchildren after a divorce. Some cut all ties with them. Such rejection can be devastating for the children involved, who will find it hard to understand. Caroline:

The children were three and five when Jeremy and I split up, and his mother – whom I'd always disliked – was really cool to me when I phoned her. She obviously thought it was all my fault. I thought she'd get better but as time went by she didn't phone up to speak to the children or get in touch with them in any way – her only grandchildren! They started saying, why hasn't grandma rung? They got so upset that in the end I forced myself to phone her up and I told her the children missed her. I thought she'd be pleased but she was quite offhand, although she did say 'Bring the children over for the day'. When I did there was an enormous picture of Jeremy with his new girlfriend gracing the mantelpiece which she'd obviously put there on purpose. It was easy to see whose side she was on, and as soon as Jeremy's girlfriend had a baby she didn't want to know my children at all.

Hostility and rejection can be hard to bear if you've always got on well – or thought you got on well – with your in-laws. Keith was shocked at his in-laws' attitude after he and his wife separated:

It was as though I didn't exist. They closed ranks against me as soon as Penny started divorce proceedings. I belonged to the same golf club as my father-in-law and if I ever saw him at the clubhouse he'd cut me dead. Yet it was his daughter who'd left me, his daughter who'd had the affair which had led to our marriage breakup. It seemed so unfair, as I'd done nothing wrong.

Keith's father-in-law felt that by being friendly to Keith he was condemning his daughter. He was blaming Keith so that he didn't have to blame his daughter. He removed the burden of responsibility from him and his family. It absolved *him* of blame.

Many of us find it hard to accept responsibility when things go wrong in our lives, and our first reaction is to try and blame others. If your in-laws – or even your parents – blame you for the failure of your marriage it's because they don't want to acknowledge that they might have been failures as parents. This is particularly true if the parents recognize inherited traits in their children which might have contributed to the breakdown of the marriage, such as meanness, bad temper, intolerance, violence, weakness or laziness. They can push aside that niggling thought which keeps nagging away at them saying, 'If I hadn't been such a bad role model perhaps their marriage would have worked out, perhaps they would have been better as a partner.'

It's not always the fault of the in-laws, however. Sometimes the injured partner in a divorce uses the in-laws to get at the estranged spouse. Tessa was devastated when her son's marriage broke down, because she'd always been close to her grandchildren.

What hurt most of all was that his wife, Wendy, whom I'd always got on really well with in the past, treated me as the enemy as well as him. There was a lot of animosity between them and although I tried not to judge him – you never know what goes on in other people's marriages, not even your own son's – I knew he was difficult to live with because he can be very moody and he drinks heavily. I tried to be as supportive as I could and let her know that. But Wendy was so concerned with getting revenge on him she tried to stop us seeing the children. This was appalling, not only for us but the children too, as they'd always been close to us; they used to stay nearly every weekend. We actually got as far as applying to the court for a contact order before Wendy finally realized how stupid she was being because the children were so upset. She rather reluctantly let us carry on seeing them. But when we pick them up she won't speak to us.

If nothing you can say will heal the breach and your in-laws cut themselves off from you and the children, explain to your children it's nothing they've done, and don't feel guilty. You've done all you can.

## LET NO MAN PUT ASUNDER

Sometimes parents or family members object to divorce because of religious, moral or ideological reasons. They interpret the Christian teaching that marriage is for life absolutely literally, and believe that having made vows to that effect a couple should stick together – no matter what.

How you deal with this depends on whether or not you were the initiator of the divorce and if you believe as unwaveringly as your parents in the teachings of your Church. If you initiated the divorce either you do not hold such fervent religious beliefs as your parents, or you interpret them differently. Although many devoutly religious people believe in the forgiveness of God there are those who are unyielding. Mark:

When Veronica and I married we were both virgins, because we came from Christian families and believed that sex was wrong outside marriage. How naïve we were – it didn't take me long to realize I'd made a mistake and that I knew nothing about her when we married. The more I discovered the less I liked her. Eventually I found out she was having an affair and felt she'd not only betrayed me by this but also our religion, which was the one thing we'd always had in common, the one thing we could share. It was impossible for me to go on living with her, and as we had no children it seemed the best thing would be to go for a divorce. But even though my mother knew that my wife had been having an affair and knew how unhappy we'd both been she thought I was wrong to divorce her. We married in the eyes of God and it should be for ever, she kept telling me. When we divorced she cut all links with me, and hasn't spoken to me from that day to this. I'm sad about it, and angry as well, because I think a lot to do with it is that she doesn't want to lose face with her church friends.

## FRIENDS: TAKING SIDES

It's a truism that you find out who your friends are when your marriage breaks down because it's a time when you need support, friendship, an ear to bend and a shoulder to cry on, and not everyone will volunteer their services. Sometimes reactions can be unexpected, and people you'd thought would back you line up against you and vice versa. Some will take sides, even those who insist they will remain impartial. Some get caught in the cross-fire: I was so convinced (wrongly, as it turned out) one of my friends was a 'spy' for my ex-husband, reporting back my every move that I refused to talk to him for six months after we split, such was my paranoia and confusion at the time.

Once you announce a separation, you free your friends from the constraints the loyalty they feel for you imposed upon them. If your partner is no longer your partner they can now say what they like about him or her. The news may well be greeted with people telling you truths they've longed to tell you for years. Caroline:

'We never liked him', someone I thought was a close friend of both of us said to me as soon as I told her. 'I can't imagine how you managed to stick it out with him for so long', she went on, and then listed all the things she hated about him. Then I found out from my sister that he'd made a pass at her, and used to sexually harass her whenever he was alone with her. She'd talked about it to a mutual friend and decided not to say anything, and I'm glad she didn't because I don't know how I would have reacted. I suppose I wouldn't have believed it – I had to find out for myself. It was in a way horrifying to hear such dreadful things about him and in a way reassuring.

At least I knew and they knew I'd done the right thing in leaving him.'

Caroline could cope with hearing negative things about her spouse because she was the instigator of her divorce and it merely proved that she was taking the right course of action. If you are the reluctant partner in a divorce, hearing bad things about your partner with whom you're probably still in love can be a great shock. Not only will you have to put up with the feelings of loss, but you'll also have to adjust to the humiliating knowledge that everyone but you knew about these things. Sometimes, however, having your illusions shattered so mercilessly can help you. Emma:

> After he went I felt gutted. I thought we'd been happy and then one day he came home and said, 'I'm leaving, I don't love you any more.' I was so shocked I hardly spoke, and he just threw some things into a suitcase and walked out. I kept saying 'why, why?' but he wouldn't tell me. The next day the police came round and I discovered he'd been embezzling thousands of pounds from his work. I had no idea where it had gone to. Then I found out he used to play poker regularly with some friends I didn't know about, and he'd gambled most of it away. He hadn't paid the mortgage for three months, he was in debt up to his eyeballs and I knew nothing about any of it. After the shock came anger – that he hadn't told me, that I'd been the last to know. He'd humiliated me in front of all these people. Knowing that made me hate him and that made it easier to accept the fact that he'd gone.

Even if the decision to separate was arrived at my mutual agreement, the partner who moves out of the family home is often blamed for the breakup by family and friends alike, simply because he or she is the one doing the leaving. Keith:

> When Penny told me she had another bloke I was devastated. I really had no idea but then I worked long hours on a farm, and I suppose she was on her own a lot. It turns out the bloke

is a so-called friend of mine, and that really finished off our marriage as far as I was concerned. She wasn't interested in trying again, anyway, otherwise she wouldn't have told me about him. She said she wanted a divorce and she wanted me to move out. This was pretty shattering because I'd done up the house myself, but I had no option because of the kids. So I moved out and for a while I kipped on a mate's sofa until I got myself sorted, and life was pretty awful. But what really hurt was that a lot of people thought it was my fault and tried to get me to go home, and I'd done nothing. I'd lost my home, wife and kids through no fault of mine while Penny was carrying on with someone and living the life of riley. I'd have been only too pleased to go home.

## WHAT FRIENDS ARE FOR

If you've had separation forced upon you and are the reluctant partner in the divorce, you'll probably receive a lot of sympathy from your closest friends. You'll need it. You're probably feeling shocked, lonely, frightened, vulnerable and emotionally confused. You're trying to find reasons why it happened, and it helps if you've got people, not so much to talk to, but to talk *at*. You don't want advice, you want a friendly, sympathetic ear so you can start unloading all the emotional baggage you've been carrying around. You want people to nod their heads in the right places and look sympathetic, and to tell you it's the best thing that could have happened. You want them to be there when you phone up late at night because you feel down and you want someone to weep to. And as time goes on and you settle into your new life as single person or parent, you'll want them to be there to give much-needed practical support, whether it's as a mate with whom you can go out on the town, a handyman – until you get the hang of DIY – or a babysitter.

## WHAT FRIENDS AREN'T FOR

Your circle of friends will probably undergo a drastic pruning as you struggle to come to terms with your new status as a divorced or separated person. You may find some of your friends aren't as welcoming to you as a single person as they were to you as a married person, and it's probably not because they are on your spouse's side, nor that they disapprove of divorce. Couples are very often caught up in a social network consisting solely of other couples, and a single person isn't welcomed or doesn't fit easily into such a circle. If you're a woman you may find that you're perceived as a threat by other (married) women, as we shall see in chapter 7.

Don't expect too much from your friends. At first you may well receive an abundance of that sympathy, support and practical help, but don't rely on it because it won't last forever. People soon start drifting away, and some may even become impatient with you, and see you as a bit of a nuisance. Expect a flurry of invites to start with, but unless you make an effort to reciprocate the invites will quickly dry up.

Divorce changes your social life. When you're young and single you tend to have close and sometimes intense friendships, but when you're married those friendships often peter out and are replaced by not-so-close friendships or even acquaintanceships with other couples. Inevitably, there will be those you won't be able to convince you're doing the right thing. Usually it's because they're looking at the situation not from your point of view but their own, and all they can see is how your divorce will affect *them*.

Don't forget, too, that your spouse may well be competing with you for the attention, friendship and support of your mutual friends. Some – even many – of these friends you probably wouldn't know if it weren't for your spouse, and some you perhaps don't even like that much. Don't worry about losing friends after a divorce. They're easily replaceable. The ones that aren't will stick by you.

CHAPTER 5

# You're Not Divorcing Your Children

> The value of marriage is not that adults produce children but that children produce adults
>
> PETER DE VRIES

In 1988-9, over 76,000 children under five experienced their parents' divorce, and it has been estimated that one in twenty-two children will experience their parents' divorce by the age of five, and one in five by the age of sixteen. Some may be involved in two or more divorces.

Once it was common for a couple whose marriage was over to stay together for the sake of the children, only to part when the children had grown up. The arguments are convincing: children are better off with two parents, they'll suffer emotionally after a divorce, they'll probably be poorer and have to live in reduced circumstances, and their relationship with the parent with whom they don't live will inevitably suffer.

## WHY AM I AFRAID TO DIVORCE?

The emotional breakdown of a marriage takes place over a period of time, and during that period the child is likely to feel the impact of his parents' crumbling relationship. Couples who are separating are usually confused and unhappy, and often they are so wrapped up with their own feelings they overlook their children's feelings. Inevitably it is the partner who doesn't want the divorce who receives all the help, support and attention, while the children's needs often are neglected. In order to get attention from their parents during this emotionally taxing time, the children sometimes have to resort to desperate measures such as displays of aggressive behaviour. *Surviving the Breakup*, a study by Judith S. Wallerstein and Joan B. Kelly, shows that the main cause of a child's suffering at the time of a divorce is because their parents are too depressed or angry to show them any love.

Sometimes it's easy to forget that even though you are getting divorced, your children are not and as far as they are concerned they still have two parents they want to love them. When a marriage is breaking down, the couple can be angry, depressed and sad. The atmosphere at home might be hostile. The children are likely to be confused, frightened, and guilty, particularly if they constantly hear their parents quarrelling. They may blame themselves, particularly if they are used by one parent to blackmail the other into staying in the marriage: 'Jamie doesn't want you to go, do you, Jamie?'

Children place an even greater strain on an already terminally sick relationship. A child who is eased through a divorce, lives happily with one loving parent and is able to visit the other parent whenever he wants, must surely be better off than the child whose parents are only together 'for the sake of the children'. That's an ideal scenario, however. Marriage breakdowns tend to be long and drawn-out, and few couples can go through them without some sort of acrimony. The decision to divorce is usually taken by one partner against the wishes of the other, and this can be difficult to accept.

Easing your children through a divorce without harming them emotionally can be difficult. It can be hard to accept that your children's needs are different from yours, and maybe even diametrically opposed to yours. Ending a marriage when there are just the two of you involved is not easy, but at least you and your partner are responsible only for yourselves. Ending a marriage where there are children involved means you must think of the children's future and what's best for them as well as what's best for you, when you're trying to come to an agreement about who will be responsible for their day-to-day care. The parent given custody of the children then has the dilemma of whether or not to look for a job and employ some sort of childcare if the children are young, or having 'latchkey' children if they are older, as few single parents are in the position of being able to afford a full-time live-in nanny.

Most divorcing couples put off telling their children they intend to separate until the very last moment, often because it seems the final acceptance that the marriage is over and all hope is gone. This is understandable, but cruel for the children. Marriages don't break up overnight, they can take years, and eventually conflict can become an accepted part of family life. Living in a home with conflict means children can grow up with distorted role models – a daughter who sees her mother being undermined by her father may grow up believing that's a wife's role in a marriage. A son who sees his father hitting his mother may grow up believing that's how husbands behave in a marriage. If they do not see their parents giving love and affection they may grow up to be unable to give love and affection themselves.

The longer it goes on, the worse effect it can have. Eventually, children who live with estranged parents come to accept their behaviour as normal. A friend of mine discovered when she was eighteen that her father had wanted to leave her mother when she was a baby and her mother had talked him into staying for her sake. 'I can remember thinking how very odd it was when I went to friends' houses,' she recalled, 'and I saw their parents kissing each other, or being affectionate in some way. My parents not only avoided touching each other, they hardly spoke. Mealtimes were a sombre occasion, and often they'd use me as a go-between. I realized that they hated each other when I was in my teens, but it wasn't until my father died that my mother told me the truth – that he'd had a girlfriend for all that time and the only thing that had stopped him going was me. I felt tremendously guilty for a long, long time because I had indirectly caused their great unhappiness.'

Children are very sensitive to atmosphere, and a prolonged atmosphere of hostility in their home can be very upsetting if they don't know the reason why. Studies have shown that the children of divorcing parents want information, but many parents fail to give explanations to their children and this adds to their misery and confusion. Even those children whose parents have consistently and maybe violently quarrelled in front of them often don't realize what's going on, especially if their parents have always had a volatile relationship. Ella remembered the shock of learning about her parents' intention to divorce when she was a child of ten:

I came home from school one day and my mother was sitting on the settee crying. I knew something was up, my father was there too, and he usually didn't get back from work until much later, often when I was in bed. I'll never forget his face, it was stiff, like a mask. He said, 'I'm sorry, Ella, I'm going to live somewhere else.' My mother jumped up and started screaming at him, 'Tell her the real reason!' Then she shouted, 'He's having an affair with someone else, that's why he's leaving us!' Of course I realize now she was so shocked and hurt she'd become almost unhinged, but at the time it devastated me. I had no idea, I'd always felt so secure, even though I hardly saw my father, as he was a hospital doctor and worked long hours. They never seemed to quarrel, I just couldn't believe it. My entire world fell to pieces. I started to wet the bed, I became very withdrawn and couldn't communicate with anyone. I think it was a form of depression because I can remember crying a lot at school, and my form teacher being very nice to me and she'd obviously told the rest of the class to be nice, too. We stayed in the same house but my mother was different. She was always unhappy and moaning about money. She turned me so against my dad I didn't want to see him until I was a bit older. Then I could understand that he hadn't abandoned me, that it wasn't his fault.

## TELLING THE CHILDREN

Once you have decided to separate, it is vital that you explain the situation to your children clearly and simply. It's a time when your children will need lots of support and, sadly, it's often a time when parents are least able to give them that support. How you break the news you are to separate to your children is crucial in how they adapt and come to terms with your separation. If the decision to end your marriage is being taken against your wishes, guard against taking out your hurt and anger on your child, as Keith did:

> When Penny told me she was leaving, I felt so wounded and angry that I did something unforgivable. Our son Simon, who was then fourteen, came home from school and I said to him, 'Your mother's having an affair with someone else. She doesn't want us any more. So I'm going to have to leave.' I cringe whenever I think about it, it had a terrible effect on him. He stayed living with her but he was emotionally disturbed for a long time, and I blame myself for being so selfish and insensitive, for using him to hurt her.

It's essential to reassure your children it's not their fault, and that even though you are separating, your love for them remains unchanged. Say something like, 'We can't live with each other any more because we don't get on, but we both still love you.' Share your feelings with them, and encourage them to express their feelings and talk about what the divorce means to them if they want to.

They don't just want information, they want reassurance. They want to know what's going on and what will happen to them. They want to be involved in making the decisions that will affect their lives – whether or not they'll have to move houses or go to new schools, whether they can still see their grandparents, how often they can see their noncustodial parent, and where he or she will be living. They may worry that their absent parent won't be able to look after him- or herself. If you involve your children in the discussion about their future from the start and encourage them to ask questions, you can dispel any anxieties they might have about their future.

## CHILDREN'S FEELINGS

How it will affect your children depends on their age, their personality, the sort of relationships they have with you, your partner and their grandparents, and how you and your partner treat the breakup. Studies have shown that children hate quarrelling parents, and are likely to suffer from low self-esteem and behavioural problems. Most children are very unhappy when their parents' marriage breaks down and may feel resentment and anger against one or other parent (often the parent they live with), especially if the divorce has meant them having to move to a smaller house, there's less money to go round and a subsequent drop in living standards. Not all, though. One study interviewed people whose parents had separated when they were children and although many were disbelieving about their parents' separation and wanted them to be reconciled, a quarter of them were actually relieved when their parents separated.

Others feel guilty and blame themselves. Some feel insecure and fearful of the future – they think, what will happen to me if anything happens to the parent I live with? Most of them are anxious, depressed, frightened and confused. They may show their feelings through tantrums, violence or truanting. Younger children may regress in their behaviour, and start bed-wetting and indulging in baby talk. Older children can be hostile and resentful. Their schoolwork may suffer. If they have to put up with a step-parent moving in and possibly step-brothers and -sisters as well, they may experience powerful feelings of jealousy.

It's important during this time to make your children realize that whatever else happens, you still love them and to show your love as much as possible. This can be hard, because the chances are you'll be feeling sad and depressed, and the last thing you need is an emotionally disturbed child giving you a hard time. Don't withhold love as a punishment. When your children misbehave, don't make them feel as though they're a nuisance and you wish they weren't around. After the separation, try and give them as much love, understanding and attention as you can. They may well behave in a very unlovable way – children who are emotionally hurt can react aggressively, or withdraw completely – but try and be understanding. They've suffered a loss too, and they're likely to be grieving for it as much as you are. Children who lack the emotional support of brothers or sisters are usually hardest hit, although older children often have to take on the responsibility of caring for younger children and older boys often have to take on the responsibility of being 'the man of the house', and this added responsibility can weigh heavily on them.

Doing what's best for the children can often be painful for the parents. Jim:

> I'd always played a far greater part in the bringing up of the children than most men because Barbara was ill a lot when they were young. Because of that even though I knew our marriage wasn't working I never did anything about it, because I just couldn't envisage living without the children. I spent such a lot of time with them; we couldn't afford help in the house but as a vicar I was home more than most men so I did most of the cooking, washing, ironing and looking after the children. I took them out, played with them and did nearly everything for them, right from when they were babies. Sometimes when things were bad I thought about separating but I just couldn't face it. It did actually make me feel quite suicidal when I thought about losing them but as time went on and our relationship showed no signs of improving I was glad to get out in the end. If the children hadn't been there I think I would have gone much sooner. I eventually came to terms with losing the children quite quickly by forcing myself to face the reality that I was no longer a father in the way I expected, but it was difficult.

## WHY AM I AFRAID TO DIVORCE?

Leaving children behind can be harder for a woman, because it goes against everything they've been conditioned into believing – that women should be prepared to sacrifice themselves and their happiness for the sake of their children. Women have been brought up to make sacrifices for those they love, and those who voluntarily relinquish custody of their children when their marriages come to an end are often reviled. Terry discovered this when she left her husband and her children as well:

> People thought the reason why I left Hugh was because I'd fallen in love with someone else, but the real reason was that I hadn't realized how unhappy I was with our marriage until I met Adrian. After we'd started a relationship I couldn't stay any longer, but there was no way I could take the children with me. Guy was three and Tina eighteen months. We lived in a cottage in the grounds of Hugh's parents' estate surrounded by fields, so they were safe playing anywhere. How could I take them away from that to living in a small flat in town? It was better for them that they stayed – they had their father and their grandparents and a lovely home. It broke my heart to do it but I thought they'd be much better off like that. People have called me an unnatural mother, and told me I should have stuck it out until they were older, but I think I would have gone mad. I really resent that sort of attitude.

Children can be better off and ultimately happier after their parents' divorce. If their parents' relationship has been particularly angry or violent, and if the atmosphere at home has been one of prolonged hostility, the peace that follows may come as a great relief. The children often receive more attention from both the remaining parent and the noncustodial parent once they're no longer living together.

Kate remembers how her loyalties were stretched by her parents during the final weeks of their marriage:

> When I look back it seems as though they were either shouting at each other or not talking at all. When they weren't talking they'd use me to run messages: 'go and ask your mother if I've

got a clean shirt', or 'can you tell your father lunch is ready.' I hated it, I loved both of them and it seemed as though they were each trying to turn me against the other one. When my father left, after the first horrendous couple of weeks things became a lot calmer and my mother and I began to positively enjoy our new relationship together.

Sometimes the children are used as pawns in a game of one-upmanship between two warring partners and their parents. Lucy:

Eleanor would arrive back from Chris's house with expensive bikes, computer games, you name it, which had been bought by his parents. As soon as my mother heard this, she'd rush out and buy something equally expensive which she certainly couldn't afford. The consequence was that Eleanor started to think that she could have whatever she liked whenever she wanted and began to play us off against each other, you know the sort of thing, 'if you won't buy it for me Daddy will, he really loves me'.

Some parents use their children to upset or gain revenge over their former partner, either by encouraging them to take sides or by instigating a custody battle, not because they feel they can offer the children a better home, but because they want to hurt their ex-partner. The phrase most usually applied to children caught in a custody battle is 'tug of love' yet this is usually far from the truth. Often these children are not the objects of love but the objects of spite, maliciousness and revenge.

It's not unknown for the children to be used as bargaining counters, too. Mike:

My ex told me she needed more money, and I couldn't afford it. I was already paying £200 a month maintenance and she had a good job, she earned more than I did. She said if I didn't pay up she'd take me to court and apply to have my access reduced, and then she'd move to the other end of the country so I wouldn't see Gemma at all. I couldn't face another battle in court – we'd had so many, so I gave in.

It's gut-wretching to have to face up to the fact that you will no longer be able to live with your children after a divorce. Only 7 per cent of men end up with custody of their children, and in the majority of those cases it's usually because there is no resistance by the mother: very few contested cases end up with the father as custodial parent. This might have made sense thirty years ago when male and female roles were clear – the father always worked and the mother always stayed at home with the children – but in a society in which more and more families have two working parents who take equal responsibilities for childcare, it's not so cut and dried and a lot of fathers get a raw deal about access after a divorce.

Bruce Liddington from Families Need Fathers, which gives advice and support to nonresident parents, feels that the judiciary is so out of touch and the Family Division the most reactionary division of law because of its secrecy. 'Nearly all litigation is heard in secret session. The law's only real accountability is public opinion, but it's this secrecy that keeps it more reactionary than other divisons of law.'

Families Need Fathers helps guide divorcing people through the difficult but inevitable emotional processes as quickly and as painlessly as possible. Says Bruce Liddington: 'When people go through these stages they're often prone to do things that could be damaging; usually when they discover they'll be the noncustodial parent. They start off contrite and emotionally disposed to holding out the olive branch, but as soon as lawyers are involved in the majority of scenarios they drive them very quickly into a state of trench warfare, which leads to a very quick breakdown in communication.

'You're in a unique position when a divorce action is started – every civil right in respect of your children, home, and income is put into limbo, you are in a state of having your civil rights and everything you hold dear suspended. This doesn't even happen to drug barons or terrorists! Once you realize this, it's easy to overreact and lose perspective. You feel very vulnerable and insecure and some people do rash things which they afterwards regret. The insecurity generated by family law is at the root of it. We prepare them for a reasonably compromising approach which is a delicate balancing act. On the one hand you have to gear that person in a way that he or she doesn't make silly mistakes or overreact, but on the other hand you want to make sure they are holding out an olive branch. We've managed to assist many people in pulling back from the brink of the abyss when lawyers push them, and re-establishing communication.'

If you're currently engaged in a custody battle, ask yourself: are you *really* concerned about the care of your children? Are you really putting their best interests first? Have you really thought about where and with whom your children would be better off living – indeed, have you even asked them? Or are you just determined your partner won't have them? Do you try and make it easy for your children by not splitting their loyalties, or do you denigrate your ex-partner to them and try and turn them against him or her, so when it comes to visiting their noncustodial parent the child doesn't want to know?

Using your children to punish your former spouse only succeeds in hurting the children. As we have said, it's a time when children need as much emotional support and love from both parents as they can get. They need the reassurance that both parents still love them, and to know that the security of their home will remain. If they are having a step-parent or sibling thrust upon them, they need to know that they are still the number one in their natural parents' affections. What they don't want is the extra strain of being employed as bargaining counters, scapegoats or objects of spite.

When your divorce becomes absolute, you will still be a parent whether or not you have custody of your children and if you are the noncustodial parent, working out arrangements for you to keep in touch with your children can be a strain. Sometimes the noncustodial parent drops out of the children's lives altogether. Perhaps they can't stand the pain of being a part-time parent, or perhaps they feel the children would be better off without seeing them, particularly if they have a new step-parent they are starting to look on as their natural parent. Wallerstein and Kelly's study *Surviving the Breakup* looked at a group of Californian children whose parents had separated and discovered that an enduring relationship with both parents is vital to the child's wellbeing, and the children who regularly saw the parent with whom they no longer lived were able to cope best with the stresses of divorce. Only in exceptional circumstances should there be little or no contact.

## HELP YOUR CHILDREN SURVIVE EMOTIONALLY

- If your ex-spouse goes to live with someone else, insist on meeting the new partner and their children if they have any, before you allow your children into their care. Are they the sort of people you won't mind leaving your children with?
- Don't use your children as pawns to get back at your spouse. If you involve them in a custody battle everyone will lose – especially the children.
- Don't encourage them to play you off against their other parent. Children are not slow to spot an opportunity, and sometimes it's tempting to let them get away with murder either because you want to win their approval as a parent or because you think they've been through such an emotionally traumatic time they deserve a break. They still need discipline from both parents, and setting limits gives their lives some sort of framework and security at a time when they are inevitably feeling very insecure.
- Don't use your children as a replacement for your spouse. Very often the children subconsciously take on the role of the missing spouse, particularly boys. Children need to enjoy their childhood, not to be weighed down with adult responsibilities.
- Don't attack your spouse in front of them – you'll make them feel their loyalties are divided.
- Keep reassuring them of your love and the love of your ex-spouse.

## MEDIATION

'The law', says Bruce Liddington, 'is full of perverse incentives to do the wrong things and the law is all-pervasive in family disputes. People who don't make contact with us or a mediation agency can very easily come to look upon their solicitor as a sort of guru instead of just a legal adviser. We try and make those who contact us not dependent on lawyers. Apart from anything else, it can end up costing them thousands of pounds.'

If there is a lot of acrimony between a couple, making the necessary arrangements about money and children can be difficult. If a confrontational approach has been encouraged by their solicitors, the antagonism between partners can become bitter and relationships between them break down completely. This is not only emotionally exhausting but as Bruce Liddington says, it costs a great deal of money in legal fees. Many solicitors encourage couples who can't work out a suitable agreement together to consult an independent conciliation or mediation service.

Couples are encouraged by the mediator to work out their own solutions to the dispute, which is usually to do with the home, finances or children. The mediator sees the couple together and doesn't counsel or offer advice or suggestions, but helps the partners end their marriage as smoothly as possible. At the time of writing, there is a Government recommendation to set up a nationwide chain of mediation centres, and to make mediation an indispensable part of the divorce process.

CHAPTER 6

# Money

*In an ugly and unhappy world the richest man can purchase nothing but ugliness and unhappiness*

GEORGE BERNARD SHAW

Sometimes couples are forced to stay together because they can't afford to part. It's an unenviable position to be in and one from which it is often hard to see a way out. During the last decade an explosion in housing prices forced a lot of young, newly married couples to take on much higher mortgages than they could afford, which in itself places a great strain on a relationship. When housing prices subsequently slumped, many couples who wanted to separate couldn't afford to sell their houses and split up, because in a lot of cases the houses were worth less than their mortgages.

New rules for legal aid, too, have made it harder for couples to get help with their legal bills in Britain, which is another reason why some of them have resisted any ideas they might have had of splitting up until the economic climate is better. If the economic revival continues, the divorce rate is expected to soar as couples are freed from their economic restraints, and are able to sell their houses.

Separation and divorce cause not only a lot of emotional problems but many practical ones as well, not least financial ones. Houses often have to be sold, furniture divided. Some couples have to pay legal bills which can run into thousands of pounds if the divorce is contested, and afterwards, one most certainly cannot live as cheaply as two. A professional couple with no children who both earn good salaries and live in a big house, drive top-of-the-range cars, and go on two holidays a year may well have to suffer a drop in their standard of living if they separate. At the other end of the scale, a couple with children who live on one salary which has to be supplemented with benefits will find it almost impossible to manage financially if they separate.

## REDUCED CIRCUMSTANCES

Couples with children often have only one wage earner – usually the husband – and he will have to pay maintenance for his children, possibly the mortgage on the marital home, maybe maintenance for his wife for a while, and also rent or a mortgage on his new accommodation. This can prove to be such a financial burden that some husbands end up living in a bedsitter or a friend's spare room or are forced to go back home with their parents, because they can't afford anything else. Many are unable to marry again unless it's to a woman who is financially independent, because if they do they'll have two homes and two families to support. Although they may earn enough to support one household, they're unlikely to earn enough to support two.

It's not as though the majority of divorced wives live in luxury on the backs of their ex-husbands, either: seven out of every ten single parents live on less than £100 a week, three-quarters depend on social security benefits, and the children of single-parent families are significantly worse off. Unless one of you is very wealthy, the chances are you will both have to take a considerable drop in your standard of living if you divorce, and unless you can both earn your living it's likely to remain like that for along time. Natalie:

> Of course you're worse off as a single parent. I'm lucky because I work from home and so I don't have to pay a child minder. I certainly couldn't live on the maintenance James pays for our son. Part of the divorce settlement meant that I took over the mortgage for our house which is about four hundred pounds a month. By the time I've paid that and the bills, the maintenance cheque and family allowance just about feeds us for the month but there's nothing left. Whenever we need anything like clothes I usually have to go with a begging bowl to my dad.

Becoming financially disentangled when you separate can be difficult, even if you've had separate bank accounts and split all the bills strictly down the middle. For the couple whose finances are almost inextricably entwined – a joint bank account, joint credit cards, car and house in joint names, the contents of the house either given as wedding presents to both or bought by both partners over the years – it can be a nightmare, and trying to divide it up can take the judgement of Solomon.

Anyone who has experienced that situation knows how petty both of you can become about possessions: some friends of mine squabbled for weeks over who would get custody of the dog (one of them, it has to be said, purely out of spite) and nearly ended up in court fighting over her ownership before common sense prevailed. The rich and famous (and sometimes even ordinary mortals) often draw up marriage contracts prior to marrying, which include arrangement for dividing the property and assets in the event of separation. But even these are not infallible, as they can be – and often are in the United States – challenged in the event of a divorce.

If you intend ending your marriage and you haven't thought out the financial repercussions, do so without delay. If you plan to leave the marital home, don't do so until you've found alternative accommodation. Those who are in a position to buy a house probably won't be able to until the existing house has been sold, which could take a long time. Rented accommodation is hard to find and you may well find yourself homeless and having to squat with parents or friends, which will only worsen your feelings of vulnerability and emotional insecurity. If your living arrangements are unsatisfactory, you're liable to enter into a live-in relationship with the first person that comes along, just to get a roof over your head – and if you do that, you may well find yourself in a similar predicament before too long.

Facing up to a drop in living standards can be difficult. Emily was advised to sell the flat she and her husband had bought after they separated, because to keep it on would mean a hard financial struggle. She resisted the idea because she loved the flat:

> We have built a nice home together and there was an awful sense of throwing it all away, of destroying it, once I'd taken the decision to end the marriage. I was worried about loss of income and how I would manage with the mortgage plus an endowment policy. The flat had increased in value quite considerably in the eighteen months we had lived there, so when we did split up we eventually agreed I would pay him the difference in value so he could put a deposit on a new house. I had to increase the mortgage to pay him off but it was only fair, as we were both working and had no children. So I surrendered the endowment and lost money on that, but it meant my monthly outgoings were reduced which helped a lot. It was a terrible struggle for ages – I lived off lentil casserole and bread for about a year – but things got better when I took in a lodger, and I managed to survive.

## REVENGE

How you handle the division of property and money after a divorce depends on whether or not you and your spouse are on good terms. If you're not, and you don't even want the divorce, you may feel vindictive when it comes to agreeing to a financial settlement. The deep feelings of hurt and anger which usually follow a separation can manifest themselves in a desire for revenge. 'I'm going to make her suffer for this'; 'I'm going to make him pay for this' – 'I'm going to take him for every penny I can'; are common threats. Some people take their revenge in imaginative ways such as cutting out the crotches of their ex's trousers, or leaving bottles of their best wine on surrounding doorsteps, along with the milk. Some do it as Mary did, by squeezing as much money as they can out of their spouses:

> My solicitor said to me, we'll take him to the cleaners, and up until then I hadn't really thought about money. But then I thought, why not? I didn't want this divorce and he's happily swanning off with this woman who's got a house of her own. He's got it made. I wanted to make him suffer, and so I went for all I could get. I stood up in court looking wan and distraught and immediately won the sympathy of the judge. I was awarded such a good settlement he came out of it with nothing.

Battles over money which involve legal advisers not only prolong the agony, they also ensure high legal bills, sometimes running into five figures. The more you have to pay the solicitors, the less there will be for you, your partner and the children. Legal bills of £20,000 are not unheard of – for settling a dispute which could so easily have been settled over a pie and a pint in the local.

According to statistics, women are usually the instigators of a divorce. One conclusion which could be drawn from this is husbands would sooner put up with an unhappy marriage than be on their own – a conclusion backed up by the fact that husbands are more likely to remarry if they instigate the divorce. Perhaps, though, the explanation is they can't afford to end their marriages. Although in law every wife has a right to be maintained by her husband and every husband has a right to be maintained by his wife, if there are children involved it's usually the husband, as noncustodial parent, who has to foot the maintenance bill.

Financial security is hard to give up and this can keep some partners in relationships they might otherwise have left. Sarah was reluctant to give up the lavish lifestyle she enjoyed as a wife:

Barry was a very generous husband, mainly I think because he thought he could keep me quiet if he gave me everything I wanted and to a certain extent he was right – I put up with his moods and tantrums and selfishness for years, because the thought of giving up my nice London flat and country house, gold card, Porsche and shopping accounts was something I couldn't bear to think about. I knew I wasn't happy, but because life was comfortable there was nothing to drive me away. He was keen to keep me happy because I was useful to him because I was good at entertaining his clients, and I suppose he cared about me in his own way. I would have gone on with this empty existence if I hadn't met someone else and started a relationship with him. He was a teacher and had absolutely nothing in the way of possessions – he had no money but he wasn't interested in them either. He asked me to live with him and I had absolutely no hesitation in giving everything up – I'd only enjoyed it all because there was nothing else in my life. Barry did all he could to do me down and if I'd pressed for it I could have had a much better settlement than I ended up with. But I didn't care about that. I was happy. Of course my life style has changed – we live in a small cottage and the Porsche and gold card went long ago – but I feel alive for the first time in years.

Money worries caused the breakup of Caroline's marriage:

I never had a day's financial security throughout the ten years I was married to Jeremy. Every so often he'd get some grand scheme in his head about writing a book, so he'd leave his job and spend the next year writing a book about some obscure health topic I knew would never get published, and of course it never was. Half the time it didn't even get finished. We'd get into debt, he'd get a job again for a while, and then the whole process would start over just as we'd got back on our feet again. While he was doing all this I had to struggle to keep us and our two children on the money I earned picture restoring. That was quite precarious because although sometimes I did well and got a lot of commissions, at other times there was nothing. Crunch time came when Jeremy borrowed money against our house to start up his own business supplying health products by mail order. It started to lose money, so he remortgaged the house, then he remortgaged it again, even though it was obvious the business was never going to make money. My fault for agreeing to it, I suppose. I should have refused to sign the final loan papers. We ended up having to sell the house to pay off his debts and I just couldn't stand any more. I left. At least now I'm only responsible for myself and the children, and I'm in control of my own finances. I can't tell you what a relief that is.

## ALONE AND IN DEBT

If a marriage breaks down because of financial worries, the chances are there's going to be a mountain of debts to deal with, the most common being mortgage arrears. If your partner has left you with a pile of unpaid bills, you won't be responsible for bills he or she has incurred alone but you will be expected to share responsibility for joint debts, such as mortgages or rent repayments.

If bills were in your partner's name it's important to contact gas, electricity, and telephone companies, tell them your partner has gone and ask that everything is put in your name. Although you'll be solely responsible for the debts in future, you do at least prevent previous debts from building up. You should also seek advice from a debt counselling agency who will help you calculate how much you owe and work out an order of priority in which to pay them. If you have a joint bank or building society account you can both draw on, tell the manager immediately and have it changed so both signatures are needed to draw out money. Put a stop on joint credit cards.

## AGREEING A SETTLEMENT

A financial settlement is reached taking into account factors such as both your ages, whether or not one or both of you has a job, how long you've been married and whether or not there are children involved. There are no hard and fast rules which say how much each spouse should get – it depends on your individual circumstances. The courts are no longer responsible for setting maintenance amounts for children (although they still do for spouses): this is now the responsibility of the Child Support Agency. The court's priority is to ensure that any children of a marriage will have a roof over their heads, and preferably the roof of the house they've been used to so that an already emotionally stressful and disruptive time isn't worsened by them losing their home. If the couple have sorted out financial and practical arrangements themselves, no formal order will be made by the court.

A wife can no longer rely on maintenance payments for life, and a young wife with earning potential is lucky to receive any maintenance for herself at all. Sometimes a maintenance order will be made for a fixed period of time to make the transition less painful, and nowadays men can claim maintenance in certain circumstances. Working out an amicable financial agreement which is agreeable to both of you and then having it legally drawn up might sound impossible if you are currently on mutually bad terms, but if you can't come to a satisfactory agreement your legal bills will soar – and the more you both have to pay solicitors, the less money there will be for you.

If there are no children and the marriage has been fairly short-lived, the court could order the house to be sold and everything split down the middle. So if, like Emily, you want to carry on living in the house you'll have to buy your partner out and come to an arrangement about the contents. If the marriage has been very short-lived, the court may divide up the assets according to who put in what – for example, if one partner earned much more than the other, paid the mortgage and bought all the furniture, he or she will receive a significantly higher share. If the marriage has been long, who paid for what rarely comes into it.

A woman who is left in the family house with children may be 'given' the house as part of the settlement, as was Natalie:

When James left he made over the house to me and I kept all

the furniture and took over the £40,000 mortgage as a once and only payment. He pays maintenance for our son, but that's it. So from one point of view he'd walked away with nothing, but from another point of view he only has to pay £100 a month in maintenance which doesn't trouble him unduly – he's got a good job now. I wouldn't have wanted him to support me, I'm capable of making my own living and I wouldn't have wanted to be beholden to him or have his resentment directed at me. The only thing I wish is that he'd sometimes buy our son some clothes when he sees him as he seems to think the maintenance is it as far as he's concerned.

When Janet decided she wanted to end her marriage she wanted a complete break, and asked for nothing – a decision she later regretted.

We had no children so I was a free agent and I just wanted out. I left with the cat and a suitcase full of clothes and left the house and all the furniture, such as it was. The house was only in his name as when we bought it I was too young for it to be put in mine. But it didn't matter; I wanted to make a clean break and I didn't care what he did with the house. In fact he sold it to a friend of his for hardly more than we'd paid for it because he was going through his socialist phase at the time and believed it was wrong to make money out of property. So neither of us got any money out of it. With the benefit of hindsight I wish I'd stayed in the house and maybe bought him out because when the pain of our separation had gone and I started to think in a more practical way I realized what I'd thrown away – especially as my wages had helped pay the mortgage.

## WHEN YOU CAN'T AGREE

If you simply can't come to an agreement about a financial settlement, make an appointment with a mediation or conciliation agency as described in chapter five. Solicitors taking a confrontational approach can often inflame the situation rather than calm it. Conciliation is confidential, and a lot cheaper and less stressful than a full-scale courtroom battle.

CHAPTER 7

# Why Am I Afraid to be Single?

Man's loneliness is but his fear of life.

EUGENE O'NEILL

You probably know at least one couple who give every impression of hating each other. You might have noticed them in restaurants, eating their meals in silence because they've got nothing to say to each other. You see them at parties, flirting with other wives and other husbands. If you're really unlucky, you've had them sitting at your dinner table where they probably spent most of the evening abusing each other, to the discomfort and unease of everyone else present.

I once knew a couple who were individually charming and good company, but whenever they were together they turned on each other with such shocking venom they became an embarrassment to be with. Everything they said to each other was calculated to wound. He usually started by making disparaging remarks about her physical appearance and comparing her unfavourably to other women. She would counteract that by telling whoever was in earshot about his supposed shortcomings as a lover. He would respond by bringing up some long ago affair she'd had, and she'd offset that by telling everyone about how he'd been passed over for promotion. She'd then finish up with a diatribe about his shortcomings as a father and burst into tears.

Everyone who was forced to witness this public outpouring of vitriol did so with mounting distaste, and when they eventually left there was a collective sigh of relief and a chorus of, 'Why do they stay together, why on earth don't they get a divorce?' I lost touch with them eventually, but as far as I know they never did.

Why some people stay in destructive relationships with partners they clearly dislike is unfathomable to those who hold more positive beliefs about marriage, but the reason is often because they prefer the insecurity of knowing the relationship is dead rather than what they see as the insecurity of having to cope alone.

Even an unhappy marriage can give you some sort of security. It's a bit like wearing a threadbare jacket: it long ago ceased to keep you warm but because you're so used to wearing it you can't face throwing it away. Sadly, some people who stay in an unhappy marriage for the security find out the hard way that no marriage is utterly secure. Your spouse could walk under a bus tomorrow, or run off with the milkman, or lose all his money. You can never predict the future.

## LIKING YOUR OWN COMPANY

Some people can't bear the thought of being alone because they dislike themselves in some way or because they have no sense of identity. Being in a long-term relationship sometimes makes us lazy: if we rely on our partner too much we can end up losing confidence in our ability to cope by ourselves. This can make it hard to become independent, as Deborah discovered when she and Glyn separated:

One of the worst things about being single again was having

to make conversation, which sounds really daft. But Glyn had always been a lot more outgoing than me and whenever we went round to friends he'd do all the talking – he was much better at it than me after all, and if I did say something he'd usually shoot me down in flames, or take the mickey out of me. When he wasn't there to do the talking and people asked me something I'd go red and be really tongue-tied. I thought I'd show myself up if I talked about politics, or things like that. For a while I never talked, just listened. It took a long time before I felt confident enough to put forward my opinion.

## FACING THE FUTURE ALONE

There have never been so many people living alone. A quarter of all households in the UK consist of only one person, and more than one in five mothers are single parents. The breakdown of the traditional family unit in which aunts, uncles, mums, dads and grandparents all lived within a stone's throw of each other or sometimes even in the same house has meant that loneliness is a very real problem to some people. The modern family is likely to be scattered all over the country, so there is little or no family support. Tower blocks have led to feelings of isolation. The demise of the corner shop has meant there is nowhere to stop and chat to neighbours. It's just not the same in a supermarket.

Loneliness is a common problem. It may be the loneliness of the single mother who is trapped at home with a young child because she is unable to work and cannot afford babysitters. Or it may be a less obvious loneliness, such as that of the man who lacks the confidence to approach others. Two and a half million people phoned the Samaritans in 1992 because they were lonely, and the possibility of being lonely is probably what most frightens people facing a divorce. Loneliness can lead to people remarrying in haste, whether or not it's right for them.

Being alone is for most people the same as being lonely. Yet this need not, should not, be the case. You can live alone and lead such a full life you're never lonely, whereas you can be lonely when you're with a group of people. Relationships can hide the fact that you're lonely, which is why so many people find it so hard to leave them. If you've ever experienced that overwhelming feeling of isolation when you're with a person you can't reach out to or make contact with, you'll know what I mean.

Natalie experienced terrible feelings of isolation and loneliness during the dying months of her marriage.

> At first James and I were going to see if we could stick together until our son was old enough to cope with us parting, although both of us knew the marriage was over. We agreed to lead our own lives and I was glad in a way because I hated the thought of being alone. But he started to behave as though he was single and expected me to stay in and look after Luke each night while he went out clubbing, and we had so many rows about it it wasn't long before we stopped talking altogether. I remember I looked at him once at breakfast – the only meal we had together – and it was like looking at a stranger. Whenever I felt sad, or hurt or in need of someone to talk to, there was nobody there. I could see him and yet he wasn't there and I felt very, very alone. I decided it couldn't be worse for me or our son if I lived alone and I've found out it isn't, because although there are times when I long for people, it's not that awful feeling of isolation I had when James was there, not speaking.

## A WOMAN ALONE

Some women have been conditioned into believing their lives are incomplete without men. The pinnacle of their achievement comes when they find a man they can marry, and the idea that it may be possible to enjoy life as an independent woman doesn't occur. As we saw in chapter 3, some women are afraid to take responsibility for themselves, which is why so many of them marry young. Their identities then become merged with their husbands – when they talk, they never say 'I', only 'we', because they haven't the confidence to express their own opinions. They become a completely passive partner, afraid of making a decision or choice, in case they make the wrong one.

It's hardly surprising. When they lived at home they were financially and emotionally dependent on their parents. If they married young, they shifted from being dependent on their parents to being dependent on a husband. If they had a job it was probably menial and unrewarding and didn't pay well. Throughout their lives they've never had to fend for themselves, never had their own identity, and never known independence.

When they married, their fathers quite literally gave them away to their husbands, whose names and identities they assumed. Their position in the community is determined by the sort of job their husbands have and the size of the houses in which they live, which is why women historically tried to find either a wealthy man for a husband, or else one whose job commanded a high standing in the community, such as a doctor or lawyer. Even though nowadays many women have good jobs and no longer need a man to be a provider, men tend to earn more than women and some women still look at a man's future prospects before they marry him, especially if they plan to have children. Women who rely heavily on their partners for status and financial support are likely to suffer from low self-esteem and lack confidence and assertiveness skills, which makes the prospect of being on their own very daunting indeed.

Carol was fourteen when she met Paul and fifteen when she became pregnant with her first baby, Kirsty. She married Paul as soon as she turned sixteen, and they lived with his parents until the council gave them a flat. She's now twenty-two with three children and unhappy, but although she wants to leave Paul she hasn't the confidence:

> I was over the moon when we first got married – I had a beautiful baby, a flat, a husband. All I wanted was for him to look after me. When I first found out he'd been seeing someone I was so hurt, I cried for days. But I forgave him and gave him another chance and we had another baby. I really thought he meant it when he said it was me he loved but since then I've found out he's had loads of other women, once when I

> was ill in hospital after having Lauren. I don't love him any more, the way he's behaved has killed it for me, and I really want out. But how can I leave? I've got three kids, the youngest three. I've never worked in my life, I've got no qualifications, I've never lived alone or had to look after myself. He's a rotten husband but he's always looked after us. I've had everything I need, never gone short. I want to go but I can't, I feel trapped. I guess the only hope I've got is to meet someone else.

No wonder Carol is scared of facing the future alone. She's had no experience of looking after herself, either in a practical or emotional way. She'd rather stay with Paul, whom she doesn't love, than be alone because she's terrified of independence and has no confidence in her coping abilities. The only way she'd contemplate leaving is if another man came along and offered to look after her, thus denying herself any chance of learning to be independent and possibly even risking a repeat of her first marriage. The way she sees it, any man is better than none.

If Paul left her and she were forced to cope on her own, it would be an uphill struggle. Society gives adequate financial assistance to single mothers, but little or no practical or emotional help. If assertiveness and confidence-building classes were offered along with welfare benefits, many women would be taught how to take charge of their lives and be able to gain true independence.

## A POSITIVE EXPERIENCE

Divorce can be a positive and liberating experience for many women, if their former partners held them back and stopped them achieving things, or if they hadn't the confidence when they were with them even to try. They do things they never knew they were capable of. They realize potential they never even dreamt they had. For a lot of women, being alone is the first opportunity they've had to take stock of their lives without having to worry about putting their partners' needs first. Would Tina Turner have achieved her position as one of the world's top female singers if she'd stayed married to her violent husband? Would Joan Collins have become the international star she is today if she hadn't been forced to earn her own living? Would Shirley Conran have become a millionaire bestselling author if she were still married to Terence? And it's interesting to see how Princess Diana has only started to develop her own personality and interests since she parted from the Prince of Wales.

Rachel was forced to take on the role as breadwinner and sole parent after her divorce. She not only responded to the challenge she flourished:

> I left Ben after years of being undermined and ground down after I discovered that he'd run up enormous debts so that the pub which was our business and our home had to be sold. Property prices had slumped and we had to sell it for much less than we paid for it. He disappeared to South Africa leaving a tangle of debts in his wake, and I was left with nothing but two teenage children. I've never been one to sit around and weep. We had nowhere to live so I rented a flat and looked around for a job so that I could get a mortgage. I'm a drama teacher but there weren't any jobs about so I applied for a job teaching English – I'd never taught English before in my life! – and managed to get it, to my astonishment. This enabled me to get a mortgage on a flat, and me and the kids moved in with hardly a stick of furniture between us. I turned out to be pretty good at teaching English and got promoted, and gradually we managed to decorate and furnish the flat. I still have to work in a bar at nights to pay the mortgage but I'm getting there. All in all I'm pretty pleased with myself that I managed to pick myself up and start over again with nobody's help. I didn't realize I could do it.

Single parents with young children have fewer options. Most are unable to work as they can't earn enough to pay for childcare, and are forced to live on state benefits and maintenance. Many live on the poverty line and can't afford babysitters, let alone the price of an evening out. Most are women, and they often lack the confidence to go out and find a new circle of friends even if they have the opportunity to do so. Mary discoverd just how hard life as a single parent can be in the months after her divorce. She'd always depended on her husband for an income, a social life and friends, and when he went she had none of those:

> After I'd spent weeks locked away in the house with the kids, getting fatter and fatter and more and more depressed, I suddenly thought, God, no wonder he left me. I'm a total dead loss. It was then I decided I was going to turn this experience into something positive, that I wasn't just going to sink into depression, live off tranquillizers and wait for old age and death. I realized I was comfort eating and so I replanned my diet and started exercising to Jane Fonda videos each evening after the kids had gone to bed. I went to evening classes and learnt how to sew, and made myself new clothes. I started to look better and feel better and that gave me the confidence to do something I'd wanted to do for ages but never dared mention when my husband was around. I enrolled with the Open University and last year I got my degree in social sciences – me, whom he always used to say hadn't a brain in my head. I've got a part-time job as a care assistant – the first job I've had for years. Soon I shall be confident enough to look for a full-time job in the social services, and the children are old enough not to need looking after. I've got a bloke but I see him when I want to. I feel in control of my life now, whereas when I was married my husband used to control my life. I can't believe I used to be the mousey wreck who sat at home comfort eating and being ignored for so long.

## COMMON WORRIES

There are 115,245 more women than men between the ages of twenty and twenty-nine. Women under the age of twenty who have no children have little trouble being absorbed back into the singles 'market' because most of their contemporaries are still unattached, but it's not so easy for older women whose friends are nearly all married. What frightens a lot of women when they're faced with a divorce is being the only single person in a circle of couples, sometimes with good reason. Patsy feels bitter about the treatment she's received from friends since she divorced her husband Tony:

> When he left it came as no surprise, in fact it was a relief. But when I thought about what life would be like being single again at thirty-six, I got really panicky. Most of my friends are married and a lot of women feel threatened by single women and think they're about to run off with their husband. Women on their own just aren't accepted. They're overlooked. Oh, I get the odd invitation to dinner parties, but only if they can invite a single man they do their damndest to get me off with. I'm an embarrassment. Everywhere you go it's couples, couples, couples – where on earth does someone my age meet anybody? I've had a couple of married men ask me out but I don't want to get into that sort of relationship. So I hardly go anywhere.

Some of Patsy's problems stem from her attitude. Because she hates being alone she probably feels awkward and uncomfortable when she's socializing, particularly if she's the only single person in a gathering full of couples, and that's what's embarrassing – not the fact she's on her own. It's a myth that single women aren't welcome at dinner parties. Anybody who is good company and has something to offer is welcome at any gathering, regardless of age, sex or marital status, and if people stop issuing invitations it's probably because they were your spouse's friends, not yours. If Patsy started holding her own dinner parties she'd ensure she'd get invited back.

The period of transition from married to single person can be a sad and depressing time if you don't let people know you're available and in need of company: sometimes friends are so afraid of interfering or being thought nosey, they're wary of getting in touch. Don't just sit there and wait for people to come to you, make an effort. Throw a drinks party, and invite all your friends, whether or not they sided with your ex, and as many new people as you can.

Entertaining is reciprocal. Hospitality breeds hospitality. If somebody asks you for supper or drinks, they expect you to invite them back. It doesn't matter if you're hard up. If you're a single parent people expect you to be hard up and they'll almost certainly turn up with a bottle. They're not there for haute cuisine but your company, and the important thing is you've invited them. It is possible for a single person to have a successful supper party, and when you've done it once you'll feel justifiably proud and your confidence will have risen by several notches.

However, a divorced woman may well be viewed by some wives as a vamp whose sole aim is to ensnare their husbands, and if she turns to them for practical help she could receive a chilly response. Perhaps there was once a jokey flirtiness between her and their husbands in the past which was acceptable while she had a partner, but now she's alone and available she's dangerous, and she can expect a distancing process to begin. It's also not uncommon for divorced women to find themselves the subject of unwanted attention from some of their friends' husbands, as Natalie discovered:

> I was absolutely astonished when one of my friend's husbands made a pass at me as soon as I was on my own. He even said he was doing me a favour! He was a real pain in the neck, always turning up supposedly to do little jobs for me and this caused so much trouble between me and his wife. I couldn't tell her the truth but she started getting suspicious and accused me of fancying him and leading him on! I don't see them any more, yet she was probably my closest friend when I was married. That experience made me very cynical about men, and about friendship as well.

## A MAN ALONE

The single man usually fares better, and often receives as many if not more invitations as he did before the divorce. After divorce he is much more likely to remarry or have a live-in relationship, partly because a lot of men can't cope with the practicalities of living alone but also because the pool of women they have to choose from is so much greater. It is far more socially acceptable for a man in his forties to go out with a woman in her twenties than vice versa, and so a single man of virtually any age is seen as a social asset. Men are usually the non-custodial parent and so have more social freedom to go out on their own and meet partners, because they're not dependent on babysitters. Furthermore, single men often attract a lot of practical and emotional support and sympathy from women who like to 'mother' men.

However, the reverse can often be true. Some think a divorced man must automatically be having a good time and enjoying his newfound 'freedom', and they overlook the fact that he might be finding it hard to adjust to life alone. As loneliness is seen as having some sort of stigma attached to it, men on their own are often reluctant to admit they're in need of company.

I once worked with a man who was in the middle of a divorce, and whenever anyone asked him how he was coping, he maintained he was having a great time. 'It's wonderful being single again,' he'd say, 'being able to play the field and go to clubs. You lot don't know what you're missing.' One day I invited him home for supper and after a couple of drinks he broke down and confessed that what really happened was he went home to a silent and empty bedsit each night and watched TV, desperate for company but at a loss as to how he could find it. He couldn't bear the thought of going to clubs alone, and all his friends had partners. He'd been unable to admit he was lonely because he thought if he did people would think there was something wrong with him. So he suffered in silence because he didn't want to lose face, and if he hadn't let his guard slip and told me the truth, he'd probably still be doing so.

## ONE CAN BE FUN

Our society is structured very firmly around the nuclear family, and there is great pressure on single people to form relationships. Because of this, a lot of people feel there is some sort of stigma attached to being single, and they dread being on their own. They don't like turning up at events or eating in restaurants alone in case people will think they have no friends they can ask to accompany them, or that they're not lovable enough to find a partner.

Because there is so much pressure on us to be part of a couple, a lot of people close their mind to the possibility that they might enjoy some time on their own and those who have to face the immediate future alone often do so with trepidation. This often leads them to enter into other relationships 'on the rebound' because they'd rather be with anyone – even the wrong person – than face life alone. Bruised by their past experiences, they seize on the first possible candidate who comes along and often end up marrying them – one reason, perhaps, why second marriages fail more than first marriages. More about new partnerships in chapter eight.

Probably most – but not all – people would rather live happily with another person than spend the rest of their lives alone, but life is rarely that idyllic and a good many of us will spend some time during our lives without a partner. If it happens to you, don't be frightened. Being alone can take some getting used to but it can be a positive and exciting time and once you get used to it you should start to enjoy the freedom it brings. Freedom to decorate your home as you want, to be able to slouch around in a dressing gown, or leave your shoes scattered on the sitting room floor, to come and go as you please, to eat baked beans out of a tin, to watch what programmes on TV you like without being sneered at, to wear what you like, eat what you like, have in what friends you like, get up when you like, live in total squalor and to make your own decisions. When you live with someone you have to forgo some of your independence and consider their needs as well as your own.

Here's a checklist:

## Living Alone: Advantages

- Independence. Being able to watch what you like on TV, eat what you like when you like, and go where you like, with whom you please.
- You discover your own identity and become a person in your own right rather than someone's wife or husband.

- No more rows. Peace at last.
- You've got a real chance of realizing your potential, and doing something positive with your life.
- Being yourself, rather than behaving as your spouse wants you to.
- Having your own circle of friends rather than your spouse's.
- Having time to do all those things you've always meant to - like writing a book or taking up a new hobby.
- Being able to live how you want, be it tidily or untidily, without being moaned at.

## Disadvantages

- Being ill and having no one to look after you.
- Coming in from work and having nobody to talk to.
- Being dropped by some friends (but that's balanced by the loyalty you'll get from others).
- Not having a regular sexual partner.
- Having no one to go on holiday with.
- Having no one to give you a hug when you're feeling down.
- Being the sole provider - what happens if you fall ill?
- Sleeping alone.

## PLAN AHEAD

Living alone and being independent takes a lot of planning. Your social life won't just carry on as it always used to before the divorce, you'll have to create a new one if you're going to be alone. If you're moving out of the family home, think carefully about where you will live. After a divorce it's often tempting to move away to a completely different area, away from family and friends, but this could leave you feeling very isolated. Keith thought it would be best for both him and his wife Penny if he moved away from the small village in which they lived, to remove the possibility of meeting each other by chance.

> There had been a lot of bad feeling between us, and I couldn't stomach the thought of going for a pint and seeing her there

> with this chap she'd got. So I decided to move away from the village where I'd lived all my life and I bought a house in town. It was only seven miles away, but it might as well have been seven hundred. I knew nobody, I missed the countryside, I couldn't get on with town pubs. I was terribly, terribly lonely and for about six months I hardly went out, just stayed in watching TV, feeling fed up and missing my children dreadfully, because I saw them only at weekends. With hindsight it was a huge mistake to move away from familiar territory: I should have stayed in the village and coped with seeing Penny with her new bloke. As it is I just made myself feel worse and only succeeded in cutting off my nose to spite my face.

Even those who actively enjoy living alone will feel lonely at times, and it would be unrealistic to pretend they won't. Your expectations have much to do with it. If you expect to be lonely, you will be. Lessen the chances of it happening by seeing being alone as a positive, not a negative, experience. Feel excited by the prospect of being able to do your own thing whenever and however you want, of making new and more rewarding relationships, of being able to create a home that looks exactly as you want it to. You don't have to fill every spare moment with things to do or people to see. Not being lonely means being at peace with yourself, liking your own company, and feeling happy and at ease and relaxed when you're on your own.

## ENJOY BEING SINGLE

Don't allow well-meaning friends to try and pair you off with partners every time you set foot in their house. Enjoy your newly found independence for a while, and don't rush to change it. The chances are you'll form a new live-in relationship at some time in the future, but you might find you like living alone so much you avoid them. Anna:

> I couldn't face the thought of sharing my lovely little flat I'd spent so long getting right with anyone again, or having to consider someone else other than myself. I like being selfish!

I like doing my own thing – I've been doing it for eight years since my divorce. When Ron said, 'Shall we move in together?' I thought about it long and hard, because I'm very fond of him and it seemed the obvious thing to do, but the more I thought about it the more I thought, 'No, I like things as they are'. He was very hurt at first but gradually he's coming round to my way of thinking. I think it's the ideal relationship – I have the pleasure of his company when I need it, but live alone.

CHAPTER 8

# Afterwards

Most of us experience a variety of emotions after a divorce including regret, guilt, anger, sadness and a sense of personal failure. What we often don't realize is that we are also likely to experience a sense of loss in much the same way as we do when someone we care for dies. The loss is different for each partner but often it involves more than just the loss of a loved one. Couples who divorce can lose a sexual partner, a companion, children, a home, income, friends and in-laws. There are a few exceptions: a couple who have taken a mutual and amicable decision to end their marriage probably feel nothing other than relief or maybe even happiness when they divorce, but in general most of us will feel a deep sense of loss.

Before you can come to terms with this loss and move on you need to go through a process of mourning, and how quickly you go through this process depends on a lot of things: if you were the instigator of the divorce; how unexpected the news was and how it was broken to you if you weren't; whether or not you are on good terms with your spouse; and if you have a loyal network of supportive family and friends to give you emotional and practical support. Much depends on the kind of person you are, and your age and background play a part. People who find it easy to express their grief and can find outlets for their feelings and who are able to share their grief with families, friends or professional counsellors, usually recover from their losses more quickly than those who shut away their emotions and hide their pain, and insist on coping without any sort of help.

Grief is a natural response to loss. It's painful but it is inevitable, and if you try and hide from it you only succeed in hiding from life itself. It's impossible, anyway, to hide forever, because your grief will make itself known in other ways, as Mary discovered:

> I was determined not to let him or anyone else for that matter see how wounded I was, how much I cared. I felt so humiliated by the way he'd left me I tried to pretend I was glad, and I buttoned up my emotions so tightly I even convinced myself. Then the panic attacks started: the first was when I was about to go to court for the first time and it was all I could do not to run home. I began to feel so bad when I was out that I stopped going out unless I was with someone else. If you've ever experienced a panic attack you'll know how terrifying they are, especially when you're in public. First the feeling of unreality, then the tightening throat and a heart that's pounding so much you're sure you're having a heart attack; then the terror begins. I went to see my doctor eventually and he was wonderful, he talked to me for ages and referred me to a counsellor who made me realize that all the pain and emotion I'd locked away inside me since Jon walked out just had to be let out, and because I refused to let it out any other way it was coming out like that.

A period of mourning gives you space and a time for reflection and healing, before you start a new relationship. If you don't grieve for your loss and acknowledge your feelings you're likely to feel insecure, lonely, worthless and rejected, and when you feel like that you're vulnerable enough to walk straight into another relationship with the first person who comes along, to ease those feelings. And if that relationship fails too, your confidence will be even further undermined.

## THE GRIEVING PROCESS

There are various stages in the grieving process. The first stage is shock and disbelief, and the extent of the shock depends on how unexpected the news was. If you are the instigator of the divorce, you're not likely to experience shock but you are likely to have difficulty at first grasping the reality of what you've done. If your partner instigated the divorce, you were probably very shocked to begin with, even if you'd known for a while that your marriage wasn't happy. If you had absolutely no idea anything was wrong, the shock can be immense. In chapter two Sally described how she thought her husband Patrick was joking when, out of the blue, he told her he wanted to leave. She simply couldn't take in what he was telling her, the shock was so great. She recalled:

> The shock was because I had no idea that anything was wrong. It was as if I'd been living a lie for all that time and it caused me to lose my confidence and question my judgement for a long while afterwards. When it finally did sink in that he really was serious, I can remember hearing this screaming and realizing it was me. Then everything went quiet and he looked at me with a mixture of fear and shame and for a while I was unable to move, I sat and stared at him and couldn't cry, couldn't do anything, I was just rigid.

After a while a new series of emotions takes over – you may feel you can't accept your marriage is finished, and when you finally do accept it you may feel very depressed. You'll probably feel angry, and this anger is usually a defensive reaction or a cover-up for sadness. You may want your partner back even if you were the instigator of the divorce. You may feel guilty, and blame yourself for all that went wrong with the marriage. Nobody's feelings are the same, but however you feel it's quite normal, and the more you express your grief the quicker these feelings will go away.

Most of us are brought up to fear outward expressions of emotion, and we're constantly urged to keep a 'stiff' upper lip. This is particularly so with men, many of whom have been conditioned not to be in touch with their emotions ('real men don't cry'), and who see any displays of emotionalism as a sign of weakness. Crying is good for you – don't be afraid of it. It helps to clear out the pain. Kate describes her feelings in the weeks after her husband Tom told her he was leaving her:

> I felt numb, as though a part of me had died, and there was this dreadful inevitability about it all because I knew that whatever I did or said, nothing would make any difference. It was rather like trying to keep afloat if you can't swim, your frantic paddling movements count for nothing but you still keep doing them because you have this instinct which won't allow you to drown without putting up a fight. The time between him saying he was going and actually moving out were a nightmare, we were both being peculiarly polite to each other as though we had turned into strangers. After he left I felt so empty and depressed, but I put on this brave face to the world, mainly because of my job. I'm a social worker, and I had to cope with other people's problems and misery, so there was no time for my own. I made out I was absolutely in control, I told friends who asked that it was the best thing that had ever happened to me and I was better off without him. Inside I felt dead, and I'd go home each night and sit and stare at the walls, hardly able to move, not eating or sleeping, just sort of frozen. Then one night a friend came round and got me talking with the help of a bottle of wine, and all this terrible anger and tears came out in an emotional torrent. It was wonderfully cathartic and I felt this strange sense of peace afterwards. I started seeing a counsellor after that and she helped me come to terms with what had happened. I wish I'd seen her right from the start because I think it would have got rid of the awful negative feelings I had that much quicker.

Eventually you'll begin to accept and adapt to your loss, and you'll know when this has happened because your heartbroken feelings are replaced by one of simple sadness and regret. This is when you start to reorganize your life and become reconciled to your loss, and perhaps feel ready to look for another partner. Most people are desperate for an affair after they've been divorced, to boost their confidence. An affair is fine, but take care the relationship doesn't become permanent. This is a time when you are very vulnerable, and it's easy to mistake sexual attraction for love.

If a divorce has been unusually bitter and full of acrimony and conflict it can be hard to rid yourself of destructive and negative feelings, which can gnaw away at you and prevent you from enjoying future relationships. Don't let this happen to you. Make an appointment with a divorce counsellor, who can help you acknowledge these feelings of aggression, resentment and anger.

Even if you know that ending your marriage was the best decision you ever made, even if your spouse abused you throughout your marriage, even if you've got a new relationship with a loving and caring partner, you'll probably still grieve. When Janet took the decision to leave her husband Rob they had grown apart so much their relationship had all but disintegrated. Because of this she mistakenly thought she'd be able to leave with her emotions still intact:

> After I left, my emotions felt on a knife edge even though I knew I was doing the right thing – I'd already left him once but allowed him to persuade me back. This time I knew there would be no going back and yet I still wept buckets when it came to it. I remember going to a party a couple of months later and my husband was there with another woman. I felt quite unreasonably upset about it, since I was with the man I'd left him for, whom I loved very much and subsequently married. I got terribly upset and one of my friends said, 'Look, if you feel like this about him what are you doing divorcing him? Why don't you go back to him?' And I started to wonder myself if perhaps I did want to go back to him, which was crazy. I'd spent ages trying to get out of this marriage. I knew

that if I wanted to, I could go back. I still had feelings for him – they don't disappear overnight. But I had another bloke I felt very deeply for, so what was going on? It was a sad and worrying and confusing time which fortunately didn't last that long. Even more fortunately, my present husband bided his time and waited patiently until I'd worked through all these emotions. When that happened I felt as though I'd been set free from the marriage and in a way I had.

You may want to end your marriage but it doesn't necessarily mean you hate your spouse. In the beginning you were attracted to that person because of certain qualities, and although those qualities may now be outweighed by other, less appealing qualities, what attracted you is probably still there.

## STARTING AGAIN

Some people mark the end of a relationship by changing things completely and breaking all ties with friends and family, even changing jobs. They have their hair cut in a new style, buy a new wardrobe of clothes, leave the country, maybe even drop out. This can be cathartic, but sometimes it can create even more problems. A friend of mine landed a job in the Middle East shortly after his divorce. Off he went, convinced this was the start of a new and positive phase in his life and that he had shut the door firmly on his unhappy marriage. But away from the support of his family and friends he found himself quite unable to cope and mix with the insular ex-patriot community, and spent most of his time depressed and wishing he were at home. He'd attempted to burn his boats too quickly, he'd tried to start again before he'd come to terms with his divorce, and four months later he came home in a worse state than he was before he left. It's usually less traumatic to ease yourself gently into a new life.

Others cope with the loss of their partner by temporarily withdrawing from the outside world altogether for a while. They feel so bruised they prefer to be alone rather than risk being hurt again. Trying to hide from reality in this way just prolongs the pain. Some simply cannot grasp the fact that their marriage is over, and live in a sad fantasy world where they wait for their partner to turn up and say it was all a mistake, or spend their time planning how they can 'win' their partner back, convinced the marriage can be saved. After a while they're likely to lose the sympathy and support they initially attracted, until one day they look round and discover they're totally alone. They need professional help or else they could remain stuck like that for ever.

## HOW CAN I MAKE NEW FRIENDS?

We saw in chapter four how divorce can change your social life, because friends tend to take sides. If you are forced to move away from your home and familiar surroundings you will have to make a new circle of friends, and the older you are the more difficult it becomes because you tend to have clearly defined ideas about the sort of people you want to befriend.

When I worked as an agony aunt for a Sunday newspaper, a high percentage of letters came from men and women of all ages who were so shy and lacking in confidence they found it impossible to make any friends, let alone meet partners. Talking to people and making the first moves towards establishing a friendship seemed an almost insurmountable obstacle to them. The reason, of course, was because they were so frightened of rejection they preferred not to put themselves in situations where there was even the remotest chance of it happening.

Life is full of risks. If you never take risks you not only have a boring and sometimes even unhappy life, but you may never succeed in finding the right partner because you'll never put yourself in the position where you're likely to meet one. Rejection *is* hard to cope with. It can seriously undermine our confidence. But it's a risk that's worth taking if you don't want to face a friendless future.

The advantage of making new friends is that they will know nothing of your past, which can be helpful when you're trying to build a new life. But it takes a lot of energy, and sometimes older people view the prospect of making new friends with dismay. You're never too old to start again. Renee:

> I was fifty when I left George. We'd been unhappy for years, but I put up with it for the sake of the kids. Then one day we were having an argument and he said, 'Why don't you just get out?' And I suddenly thought, why not? Our youngest son was eighteen, there was nothing to keep me there any more. Most of our friends were his friends he'd made from the pub, there was nobody I could count on as my friend, nobody I'd miss. So one day when he was at work, I left. I knew I couldn't have done it while he was there. My son helped me move and I moved in with my mother, who lived about seventy miles away, until I could find a place of my own. I knew nobody there except her. I had to create a whole new life for myself in a new town, and it wasn't easy. It took time. I joined everything I could – a political group, the local bridge club, WI, the history society. I forced myself to go out and take part in anything that was going, even though my natural inclinations were to stay at home by the fire with my dog. Gradually the invites started coming – and kept coming. Twenty years later I'm a parish councillor, I've got dozens of good friends, I play bridge regularly, I work in a charity shop and there's always something going on every weekend. I'm totally happy being on my own.

Meeting new friends and rebuilding your social life doesn't happen by accident. It needs careful planning and not a little effort – effort you might not feel like giving at the moment. Take it gently. Start by going through your old address books. When we're single we often have close friendships with other single people, but those friendships tend to be weakened or fade away altogether when we marry, because we invest all our love in our partners and children. If any of your old friends are still single, get in touch with them. Let them know you're available.

## YOU CAN DO IT!

Nobody is born a skilled communicator. It takes time and practice to learn the art of conversation, and it comes more easily to some than others. But it's something you'll have to learn if you're going to be on your own, because you won't be able to rely on a partner to do it for you. Those of us confident and relaxed enough to walk into a party alone and immediately start a conversation are in the fortunate minority: most of us feel awkward and ill at ease when we're in a group of strangers, without the security of a partner at our side.

Lack of confidence is a major reason why so many of us find it difficult to communicate. The happier you are with yourself the less you'll care about what people think of you, and so you'll be relaxed in company. Those of us who lack confidence, though, are so anxious to make a good impression when we meet people that we become nervous and self-conscious. Our minds go blank. We become tongue-tied and think we must be boring people. Social occasions become a nightmare.

If your spouse was confident, extrovert and outgoing, you probably didn't have much chance to practise your conversational skills. I used to be married to one such man. His powers of rhetoric were such he could convince anybody listening to him that black was white. He hardly paused to draw breath once he really got into his stride, and he generally had a circle of admiring people either hanging on his every word or arguing the toss with him. As a result I not only had little opportunity to put forth my point of view but my confidence became seriously undermined, because I felt I couldn't compete with such effortless verbosity. I thought I had nothing to contribute. I lost confidence in myself and my beliefs and ideas. 'Why don't you ever say anything? Are you stupid?' he'd ask me over and over again. Apart from the fact I could hardly get a word in edgeways, I used to wonder why anyone would want to listen to what I had to say when they could listen to him. So I kept my mouth very firmly shut. It wasn't until long after he and I had divorced that I learnt to hold a converation, and found the confidence to put forward opinions on subjects I'd previously left to him. Now there's no stopping me! But I wonder what I'd be like if I were still with him?

A checklist:

## Tips on Handling Conversations

- Don't wait for people to approach you – make a real effort to talk to people wherever you are
- Listening and showing you're interested in what the other person is saying is an important part of conversation
- Ask people about themselves if the conversation starts to flag – it's the one subject on which everyone is qualified to speak
- Smile when you meet someone and keep eye contact when you talk to them
- Read newspapers or listen to news programmes, so you've always got something to talk about

## MARRY IN HASTE...

After a divorce most people want an affair to boost their confidence, but some actively seek another permanent relationship, particularly men. About half of all divorcees remarry within five years of their divorce and many more live with a partner on a permanent basis. Some go into relationships 'on the rebound', before they've properly come to terms with the loss of their previous partner, and this can be disastrous, as Sally discovered:

> I felt so lacking in confidence after Patrick went because I felt such a fool that I hadn't realized anything was wrong. I loathed being on my own and I was terrified at the thought of having to chat someone up, so when I met Richard at a party my friend persuaded me to go to and we got on well, I just clung to him. I suppose I thought that because he seemed a nice enough bloke and he was available, he'd do. We married not long after the divorce became absolute, but things started to go wrong from the start because my children never liked him and although they're grown up and don't live at home I felt

my loyalties were being stretched. I see now I was looking for a replacement for Patrick because I hadn't got over the divorce. I wanted Richard to be like Patrick was when I first met him so I could pretend the divorce had never happened, and of course he couldn't and I don't think our marriage will last.

We saw in chapter seven that there's a lot of pressure on single people to form relationships, so much so that meeting someone else is often the first thing people think about after they divorce. Don't rush it – there's nothing wrong with being on your own for a while and it's important to finish one relationship before starting on another. Don't let yourself be carried into a new and hasty relationship before you've properly ended the last. If your divorce was a particularly wounding experience, being on your own will give the wounds an opportunity to heal.

You'll probably have some well-meaning friends who try to push you into a new relationship before the ashes of your marriage are properly cold. Resist them. Get yourself sorted first, build yourself a new and independent life and learn to enjoy your own company. Get to grips with the problem areas in your life and become self-sufficient before you start thinking about another relationship. See what it's like to be on your own. You might like it. If you've given yourself some breathing space, if and when you eventually feel ready enough for a new relationship you'll be more aware of the potential pitfalls and better equipped to deal with them.

Meeting new partners is easier than most people think. Most couples meet via work, friends or colleagues, so let everyone know you're available. Another good way to meet partners is by joining clubs which cater for your particular interests – sports clubs, drama groups, rambling groups, history clubs, gardening societies, political clubs, you name it. Most towns have clubs which cater for every interest and taste. Voluntary work is also a good idea because it brings you into contact with different people, and helping others is good for the self-confidence.

## REMAINING FRIENDS AND BREAKING AWAY

Divorces are stressful and emotionally hurtful, and many people find it hard to imagine that they can ever be on good terms with their former spouse. Time dims memories and heals wounds, however, and if after a period of time each partner has managed to come to terms with the divorce they can forge a new and relatively civilized working relationship with each other. Graham's divorce was six years ago and he and his ex-wife Annie live near and see a lot of each other because of their ten-year-old daughter Sophie. After an initially stormy start they now get on reasonably well, although Graham believes Annie exploits him:

> For Sophie's sake I go along with whatever Annie says, although it's cost me a lot of money. I think she exploits the fact that I adore Sophie so much I'll do anything to keep things happy between us. I only live near her so Sophie can come and stay with me each weekend, and sometimes during the week if Annie's going out. Once she asked me for a couple of thousand pounds to buy a car she wanted and I told her I couldn't afford it. A week or so later she said she was thinking of moving to the other side of the country. I bought her the car. I think she was only trying it on, but I couldn't take the chance of her moving, because I wouldn't be able to see Sophie when I wanted. We're only really on good terms because I give in to her the whole time.

After a divorce a lot of couples feel as though they never want to set eyes on each other again, but if they have children it's impossible to break away completely. It makes sense, then, to try and dispense with the enmity and establish a reasonably amicable relationship, because there will be times when you need to talk about your children's future needs, and as you will be linked together via the children until they are at least sixteen, it could be many years before you can break free entirely.

Some people will never be able to do this, because they won't allow themselves to accept that their marriage has failed. They're unable to move on and stay rooted in the past, their anger and resentment stoked whenever they detect any sign of happiness in their former spouse's life. Not for them the fulfilment of a second, happier marriage: even if they marry again they're unlikely to be able to rid themselves of the hatred they feel, and so the odds are stacked against their second marriage. This resentment and hatred is a form of emotional attachment. Richard:

> We've been divorced for ten years, she's married someone else and got a couple of kids and yet she still hates me so much she won't let me have back personal things which are mine – photographs, memorabilia, that sort of thing, which are meaningless to her. I cannot understand how she can feel so mean-minded after such a long time. I can only think that because love is so akin to hate she must still have feelings for me.

The emotional attachment that binds you to your ex has its roots in the past. It's no longer relevant but it provides security, and it's often hard to cast that aside. Breaking away can be hard. I'd been apart from my ex-husband for three months and by then we were on reasonably friendly terms. Occasionally he'd turn up at my new flat if he wanted a bed for the night, or a meal, and I found it difficult not to fuss over him. He was going for a job interview and hadn't anything suitable to wear, so I bought him a new suit because he was broke and I still felt responsible for him, even though I didn't want to live with him any more. This did neither of us any good because he kept turning to me whenever he was in a fix and of course I'd help him out, and the emotional attachment we had for each other only really broke when we each found new partners.

Until you can break that emotional attachment, you'll find it hard to move on. Richard's former wife has a new husband and family, yet she still allows herself to waste valuable energy hating him. If she managed to draw a line and properly end their marriage she'd be at peace at last and able to get on with the rest of her life. Graham managed it, even though he lives near his ex-spouse and still sees a lot of her:

Annie's in a special position because we share a daughter, but apart from that she's just another person and she'd no more come running to me when she had a problem than I would to her. We have absolutely no emotional dependency on each other. It took a few years to come to this point and at first there were a lot of sad memories when I used to remember how happy we'd once been. But then I'd think about the bad times, the rows and quarrels and disagreements, the pain when I realized our marriage couldn't be saved. And that helped me gradually to cut loose emotionally.

Some people end up marrying facsimiles of their former partners for the same reasons. Learning to be independent is the best way of breaking the dependency. That means:

- Having the confidence to make your own decisions, without phoning your ex to find out his or her opinion
- Taking risks. If the thought of doing something frightens you, go ahead and do it. I'll repeat it – people don't tend to regret the things they do, but the things they *don't* do
- Managing your own money. Even if you live on state benefits, if you can learn to budget and manage your money, you'll have taken an important step towards independence
- Learning a skill or taking up a new hobby, preferably something you didn't have the confidence to do when you were married
- Doing what you want to do at all times. You're on your own now
- Letting your ex-spouse solve his or her own problems

The bonds can still remain even though the partners move away or remarry. They can even be reunited, albeit temporarily, if a tragedy occurs which they can both share. An example is a couple whose two-year-old son was murdered. This terrible tragedy took its toll on their relationship which finally gave way under the strain. The wife, worn down by the emotional strain, sought solace with her former husband because there was still an attachment between them and she believed only he could understand and empathize with her during that sad time.

## NEW RELATIONSHIPS

Some people end their marriages because they've met someone else with whom they'd rather be. Perhaps they've been having an affair with that person while they were married, which immediately makes their relationship even more exciting and dangerous because it's illicit. They fall in love, and a decision is made to end the marriage. They're in love and so they move in with each other straight away, because there doesn't seem to be any point in waiting. How can there be problems, they ask themselves, if two people are in love?

The answer is: quite easily. Making a smooth transition from one relationship to the other can be difficult, particularly if you don't allow yourself a little breathing space in between. As we saw earlier, it's often necessary to mark the end of a relationship with a period of mourning before you can properly begin again even if you're the one who wants to end it.

Your relationship will no longer be an exciting, illicit affair. it will have to adjust to the reality of day-to-day life and the problems that can bring. Your income may well be considerably reduced because you're maintaining two families, and this can cause a lot of pressure. If there are children there may be battles with ex-spouses over maintenance and access, or perhaps the children are living with you which causes extra strain on a new relationship. It *can* work well, especially if there are no children, but going straight from one relationship to the other without giving yourself space and a period of reflection can be dangerous. You haven't given yourself any time to be yourself and to think about what went wrong, and how to prevent the same problems from occurring.

Men are often thought of as being more emotionally self-sufficient and able to cope with a divorce more easily than women, but the reverse is true. Research has shown that men feel a very deep sense of rejection and hurt pride, and many of them find it hard to cope with the day-to-day practicalities of living alone. They feel insecure and in need of reassurance afterwards, and are far more likely to rush into another live-in relationship soon after a divorce than a woman. The scars can run deep, as Graham found out:

> Despite the fact that I have a marvellous second marriage of five years standing, I still get nightmares about broken relationships. But it's possible I'll never feel secure and this is something I'll have to live with. Very occasionally when I have a row with my partner I think to myself that the whole awful divorce process is going to happen again. It's her second marriage too, and she shares these fears to a certain extent. But I think we have both arrived at the stage of understanding that when we do have a row it's not the end of our relationship and we'll be friends again soon.

If you have never come to terms with the failure of your first marriage it can cause problems in the second. If you can learn from the experience and understand the reasons why your marriage failed, you'll be better equipped to deal with relationships in the future.

There is a high rate of failure among second marriages. No studies have been done which can say why, but a major reason must be because so many people marry in haste after a divorce because they dislike being on their own. Think hard if you're contemplating remarriage. Ask yourself – are you marrying for the right reason?

- Do you hate living alone?
- Do you have an overriding desire to be looked after or to look after someone?
- Are you insecure?
- Do you have money problems?
- Do you feel your children would be better off with a stepparent?

If you've answered yes to all these questions, hold on before you rush into remarriage. Sit back, relax and try to enjoy being alone for a while. Feel what it's like. You're probably so scared of being alone you've never allowed yourself to experience just how satisfying it can be at times. Live with your new partner if you must, but don't be in a hurry to remarry.

## STEP-PARENTS AND CHILDREN

Don't use your children as an excuse to rush into a new relationship. Their standard of living may well be lower than a lot of their friends who live in two-parent households, but the chances are they'd rather that than have a step-parent and maybe step-brothers and sisters foisted on them.

Few children welcome a step-parent, even if some come round to the idea after a while. Children who live with single parents often have very close relationships with that parent, and they may well be jealous of a step-parent's claim on their parent's time and affections, and resentful that the step-parent has taken the place of their absent parent. They are likely to resist any authority from the new step-parent, particularly as children living with single parents often have a more free and easy existence than those who live with both parents.

Becoming a step-parent or making your child a step-child is so important it's crucial not to rush into it. Think very hard before you embark on such a major undertaking. Children feel hurt and angry when their parents divorce, and if a step-parent arrives on the scene they often direct their anger towards them rather than their own parents. It can put a strain on the relationship as the natural parent tries to please both the child and the new partner.

At the start of a new relationship a couple is still in the process of finding out about each other, and there will be plenty to talk about. You'll probably want to be alone together as much as possible and your children may feel in the way, and children who feel pushed out may try and undermine your relationship as much as they can. You're not just developing your relationship with your new partner, but with his or her children as well. Often this means a lot of demands on your time. Lisa:

When Tim and I got together his three children were deeply traumatized, their mother had left and she'd taken them, found she couldn't manage with them and so she dumped them. Imagine how rejected they must have felt. The oldest was only ten, the youngest three. When I moved in with him I took my two boys with me, whose ages fell in the middle. We tried to involve all the children in our courtship, we tried to love all of them so nobody felt left out. It helped that he has three girls and I have two boys – maybe if they'd all been the same sex there would have been more competitiveness, more jealousy. But they all get on fine and I've just had a baby and that seems to have cemented everyone into a huge extended family. Of course we've no time for ourselves. We've never been anywhere without the children and sometimes I wonder what it'll be like when they grow up and move away. But he's a good, kind man and the children bring us so much joy it makes up for not being able to have time for ourselves.

Most people aren't that lucky. Children can manipulate, undermine and ultimately destroy a relationshp between their parent and new partner, as Natalie discovered when she moved in with Guy a couple of years after her divorce.

The main cause of all the rows was discipline. I used to resent it when Guy told off Shaun – I thought it should be my job, as he was my child. Guy disagreed. He thought that as he was living in the same house we should both have the same rights over him. Shaun resented him like mad because he saw him as taking his father's place, and he was a real pain in the neck. Most of the time he spent looking sullen and even though I tried to give him as much fuss and attention as possible I couldn't seem to reach him. He talked about his father nonstop, although his father had never done anything for him, he was doing it to get at Guy. I put up with all this because I knew how upset he was but at the same time I wanted our relationship to work. Then one day he cut up Guy's collection of antique cigarette cards and that finally succeeded in breaking us up. Guy was so furious I thought he was going to do something violent to Shaun and I had to protect him. So he started accusing me of being a rotten mother because I let him do as he liked – well, it went on from there. We never quite recovered from that row and it was obvious after that that Guy didn't just dislike Shaun, he loathed him – and I'm afraid the feeling was mutual. We parted company soon after.

Don't think your child would be better off if you remarry because the reverse is often true. Bear in mind that if you and a new partner get together it's because you are attracted to each other, but your children will be thrust into the relationship whether or not they care for their new step-parent. There may be friction and rivalries with step-siblings, and feelings of jealousy and resentment if a new baby arrives. Even if they get on reasonably well with their step-parent, they could find their loyalties compromised: the arrival of a step-parent effectively ends all hope the children might have had of being able to get their parents back together again, and if that step-parent is living with the father or mother they only get to see at weekends they may see the step-parent as the person who has deprived them of their parent, which will cause even more resentment.

If all this sounds unduly pessimistic, take heart. Although divorce is a distressing and depressing experience, and for some, the scars never quite fade, it need not be the precursor of a lonely future. If you learn from your former mistakes and don't rush headlong into a new relationship before the curtain has fallen on your first one, it can be the foundation on which you can build a successful and happy second marriage. After all, divorce makes you aware of what can go wrong with a relationship, and armed with that sort of knowledge you're better equipped to ensure that history doesn't repeat itself.

# Useful Addresses

British Association for Counselling
1 Regent Place
Rugby
Warks CV21 2PJ

Catholic Marriage Advisory Council
196 Clyde Street
Glasgow G1 4JY

Children Need Grandparents
2 Surrey Way
Laindon West
Basildon
Essex FS15 6PF

Church of England Children's Society
Edward Rudolph House
Margery Street
London WC1X 0JL

Families Need Fathers
BM Families
London WC1N 3XX

Family Mediators Association
The Old House
Rectory Gardens
Henbury
Bristol BS10 7AQ

Gingerbread
35 Wellington Street
London WC2E 7BN

London Jewish Marriage Council
23 Ravenshurst Avenue
London NW4 4EL

London Marriage Guidance Council
76a New Cavendish Street
London W1M 7LB

Mothers Apart from Their Children (MATCH)
c/o BM Problems
London WC1N 3XX

National Council for One-Parent Families
255 Kentish Town Road
London NW5 2JT

Northern Ireland Marriage Guidance
76 Dublin Road
Belfast BT2 7HP

Parentline Opus
Rayfa House
57 Hart Road
Thundersley
Essex SS7 3PD

## USEFUL ADDRESSES

RELATE
Herbert Gray College
Little Church Street
Rugby
Warks CV21 3AP

Scottish Marriage Guidance
105 Hanover Street
Edinburgh EH2 1DJ

National Step-family Association
72 Willesden Lane
London NW6 7TA

Women's Aid
PO Box 391
Bristol BS99 7WS

# Further Reading

*Remarriage* by Helen Franks (Bodley Head 1988)

*Get Rid of Him!* by Joyce Vedral (Fourth Estate 1993)

*You're Divorced But Your Children Aren't* by T. Roger Duncan and Darlene Duncan (Prentice Hall 1979)

*Voices In the Dark* by Gillian McCredie and Alan Horrox (Unwin 1985)

*Children In the Middle* by Ann Mitchell (Tavistock 1985)

*Mummy Doesn't Live Here Any More* by Helen Franks (Doubleday 1990)

*A Woman In Your Own Right* by Anne Dickson (Quartet 1982)

*Happy to Be Single* by Liz Hodgkinson (Thorsons 1993)

*Divorce and After – Fathers' Tales* by Mary McCormack (Optima)

*Divorce and Your Children* by Anne Hooper (Unwin 1983)

*Surviving the Breakup: How Children and Parents Cope with Divorce* by Judith Wallerstein and Joan Berlin Kelly (Grant McIntyre 1980)